Brazilian Jiu-Jitsu

NO HOLDS BARRED!

FIGHTING TECHNIQUES

Rodrigo Gracie
and
Kid Peligro

INVISIBLE CITIES PRESS • MONTPELIER, VERMONT

Invisible Cities Press
50 State Street
Montpelier, VT 05602
www.invisiblecitiespress.com

Library of Congress Cataloging-in-Publication Data

Gracie, Rodrigo.
No holds barred fighting techniques / Rodrigo Gracie with Kid Peligro.
    p.   cm.   -- (Brazilian jiu-jitsu)
ISBN 1-931229-40-6
1. Jiu-jitsu--Brazil. I. Peligro, Kid. II. Title. III. Series.
GV1114.G743 2005
796.815'2--dc22
                            2005008653

Anyone practicing the techniques in this book does so at his or her own risk. The authors and the publisher
assume no responsibility for the use or misuse of information contained in this book or for any injuries that may
occur as a result of practicing the techniques contained herein. The illustrations and text are for informational
purposes only. It is imperative to practice these holds and techniques under the strict supervision of a qualified
instructor. Additionally, one should consult a physician before embarking on any demanding physical activity.

Printed in the United States of America

Book design by Peter Holm, Sterling Hill Productions

I dedicate this book to my father, Reylson Gracie, a great teacher and an even better person, for all he has done for me. Thanks also to my wife Laura and my kids Erica and Joao for all the love and happiness they bring to my life; to my cousin Renzo for his great teachings; to my uncle Royce for being a friend and for helping me when I needed it the most; to my conditioning coach Martin Rooney for all the training; and to all my friends and fans for their unwavering support.

Contents

Ground Fighting / 109

Closed Guard / 111

Open Guard / 141

Passing the Guard / 165

Introduction

No Holds Barred fighting is the ultimate test of skills. It is just you and your opponent in the ring, with a minimum of rules, matching strength, speed, and technique against each other. It is the closest thing to the ancient battles between gladiators that you are likely to see. It is the sport I have devoted my life to.

The new popularity of NHB began more than a decade ago, when my cousin Royce Gracie utilized Gracie family techniques to defeat larger and stronger opponents in the original Ultimate Fighting Championships. The world was shocked, and thought they were seeing something brand new, but actually it was a moment my family had been training for decades. Gracie jiu-jitsu was developed by my family as a way for a smaller person to defeat a larger person in a physical confrontation. For over 75 years my family has been testing these techniques. My grandfather Carlos, great uncle Helio, and their sons fought many a street fight and professional fight with the objective of perfecting the techniques that worked and discarding the ones that didn't. As my family proved throughout the 1990s, Gracie jiu-jitsu is still the best preparation for any NHB fight.

As a child, I learned Gracie jiu-jitsu, too. To me, being a Gracie means being ready to step up to a challenge at any moment. I am a part of a tradition. That tradition has been kept alive by the sweat and blood of my uncles and cousins, and now it's my turn. And when I am done, the next generation will take over.

Since I've been fighting as an adult, the World of NHB has expanded tremendously. Nowadays NHB fighters must have knowledge of Gracie jiu-jitsu techniques to survive in the amateur and professional arena. Whereas originally fighters would come to NHB events representing their martial arts style, with very little knowledge of another martial art, today NHB fighters needs to be well versed in some form of grappling, takedown, and striking arts. Today's typical NHB fighter has a background in Gracie jiu-jitsu, wrestling, and Muay Thai or boxing. I vary my training regimen depending on my opponent, but a general training schedule for me mixes conditioning, wrestling, Muay Thai, and Gracie jiu-jitsu.

Gracie jiu-jitsu forms the foundation of my fighting style, and thus the foundation of the techniques I will teach you in this book, but jiu-jitsu alone is not enough in the NHB world. Since NHB fighters can use a limitless number of attacks and submissions—including chokes, armlocks, kicks, and punches—NHB techniques have to be specialized. Because of

The kind of fighter who, when hit, fights back! Pride Bushido, October 2003. Luca Atalla photo

the threat of strikes, the techniques have to be modified to take into account being able to strike your opponent or being able to protect yourself from your opponent's fist. Some of the techniques that work for sports jiu-jitsu and submission grappling have to be discarded or modified. In this book, I concentrate on the techniques with special effectiveness in the NHB arena. I have selected a range of techniques that will give you a basis to develop your game from, so start practicing and expanding your possibilities. Since the ultimate goal of any fighter is to submit his opponent, I have selected many of my favorite techniques that end with a submission. I have also tried, whenever possible, to link up one technique with another, so you have a sequence of techniques that work as the fight progresses.

In selecting the techniques for this book, I wanted to present a complete game. I have selected a few things that I prefer from each of the fighting elements. Of course I cannot present everything that I use in one book, but I tried to include a well-rounded selection so that anyone, regardless of NHB experience, would have a base to start from. I took into account that some people want to learn just enough techniques to win a street fight, but I also wanted to include advanced techniques so that even experienced fighters can benefit from this book.

The moment of truth: You are all alone when the fight starts! Rumble on the Rock 6, November 2004. Kid Peligro photo

I believe I have covered all the most important aspects of fighting. When using this book, if you are an NHB novice, try to use the techniques as the basis to develop your fight game. Intermediate and advanced fighters should look at the techniques I present and decide how they can best fit them into their game.

NHB fighting is not for absolute beginners. It's too dangerous. In this book, I assume that you've already mastered the basics of Gracie jiu-jitsu and are proficient enough to be able to defend basic attacks and escape situations, such as the mount and the opponent taking your back. In addition, you should have knowledge of base, guard passing, takedowns, striking, and other parts of the top game. If you don't, go learn the jiu-jitsu basics before tackling the techniques in this book, and definitely before stepping into the ring with somebody who is trying to knock your block off.

It is important to remember that NHB is the ultimate sport, the closest thing to the primordial ways of survival, two men fighting to conquer each other in battle. Because of that, the stakes are much higher. Success and failure cut much deeper than they do in sport jiu-jitsu or submission grappling, so the training and the mental preparation are extremely important. It is not just necessary to master the techniques and be able to execute them against your partner. It is also necessary to harden yourself, to have the proper emotional control so that you can remain calm and think clearly even at times when your opponent is delivering strikes with the intent to put you out!

To that end, in the first part of this book we will go over the training and preparation that is required to perform at the incredibly high level of NHB, paying particular attention to the mental game and fight preparation. In the remainder of the book, we will focus on the techniques.

I hope you enjoy the book, and I hope it brings your game to a higher level than you ever could have imagined.

Mental Preparation

Winning an NHB fight is the ultimate rush. There's simply no experience like it. When you win, you feel as if you are reborn. Prior to the fight, you see your proud opponent looking at you with the fight face, and when you break him it feels good. It's an ego thing. It's a battle of spirits as much as it is a physical battle, and when you win, it means your spirit overcame your opponent's spirit. But nobody wins every fight, and believe me, when you lose, it feels as if your spirit died. Your pride is broken. A mature fighter needs to learn how to deal with losing as well as winning, because both can be emotionally overwhelming. That's why I consider mental preparation as important as physical.

In a big match, when you get on the stage and are about to get in the ring, the adrenaline and excitement are awesome. It is important to learn to focus and control that excitement, to turn that into energy for your fight and not let it consume you. The most successful fighters are the ones that harness that excitement and turn it into desire to fight, desire to win.

How do you do that? Well there's no one formula. It is different for each person. Experience helps. The more times you are faced with a situation like that, the more used to it you will get. The ability to transform the nervous energy into fighting energy increases with each fight. It is important, especially in the beginning of your career, to properly develop your growth as a fighter and not get into situations you aren't ready for. Do not follow my example! Because my last name is Gracie, I was quickly entered in big shows. I had to learn on the job against top-notch opponents in front of thousands. Thanks to my upbringing and the techniques I learned from the time I was very young, I was able to deal with the situation and even thrive on it. But given the choice, the proper career course is to progressively increase your opponent level with each fight.

Take the example of boxing. Up-and-coming fighters are fed easy fights in the beginning, and the opponents get harder as they win and progress. By fighting easier fighters, you develop your confidence. You become more and more comfortable with the ring, the crowd, and the excitement of fighting. In addition, you have a much better chance of surviving a bad outing or a mistake against an easier opponent. If you are fighting a top fighter, any mistake you make may be the end of the fight.

This is the same thing as when you are trying to learn a new move. You need to start practicing it against lesser partners, so that you can err and recuperate and repeat the move over and over until you get the nuances down. Once you have mastered the new technique, you can try it against tough opponents. If you try to use a new move against the top guys in your school, since you don't have the mechanics down, you may not execute it properly, and then you may not have another chance, because your opponent is too skilled. After a few frustrating times, you will give up on the move and simply think it doesn't work. But in reality, you simply did not allow the proper time and conditions for the move to mature in your game and in your mind.

As you progress in your fighting career you will learn what it takes for you to react properly under different circumstances. It is different for each person. Some people are naturally excited and want to get in the ring and fight right away. They spend a lot of their energy just wanting to fight.

Other people are worried and spend their energy worrying about what is going to happen. Will I flinch when I get hit? Will it hurt? Am I ready? Is he better than me? Others are cool and remain perfectly calm—many times too calm for their own good. They get in the ring without being energized enough to fight well.

For each style of fighter, there are some pointers that can help. If you are the type that spends all your energy prior to the fight anxious to brawl, you need to focus on something to calm you down. Think about the training that you did, talk to your coach or sparring partner and go over strategy or a specific move that you'd like to employ. Go over details of the move and when the best situation is to use it.

If you are worried about the fight and your reaction when in the ring, it is best to focus on things you can control and take your mind away from the unknown. Think about the moves that you like to do. Go over them in your mind in great detail. Think about how it felt the last time you pulled the move on someone. Focus on how you felt the last time you succeeded and won a fight. Think about the quality of training and instruction that you had from your team. How hard you worked, all the hours in the gym, all the sweat you put out and sacrifices you made, and how ready you are for this fight!

Are you willing to risk everything? Rumble on the Rock 6, November 2004. Kid Peligro photo

If you are the type that is too cool and has a hard time getting up for a fight, then you should think about fighting. Start running through your mind the first few minutes of the fight. Think of yourself walking down the path to the ring, getting into the ring, your opponent staring at you, ready to exchange leather. The referee saying, "Let's get it on!" You walking towards your opponent and the fight starting. Go through a few scenarios and get fired up!

When I look at my opponent on the opposite side of the ring, I always think, "You bastard! I'm going to beat you up because of all the pain I have been through in training, sparring, conditioning, traveling, and being away from my family. Someone is going to pay for all the sacrifices I have made, and it's going to be you!"

During your early fights, when you get into the arena, it feels like you are having an out-of-body experience, like you are looking at everything from above. At my first fight in Vanderbilt, I only came to my senses and realized that I was in a fight when we got to the ground. At that point I felt my spirit come back to me. We started and it looked like I was watching from outside. Then I took him down and the dream ended and I woke up and I was on top of him. My second fight was in Pride, against Matsui. Again, it felt like I was watching from outside. About the middle of the round I started getting more focused. It was like my soul got back into my body.

When I get to the big entrance at a big show, and the crowd is going crazy, I use that to relax myself. When I jump in the ring and I look in the corner and see that everyone is so concerned about me, that calms me down and gives me a lot of comfort. I feed off the energy of the people. When you are there and the crowd goes crazy you really feel it. It's very emotional. At that point in a fight, it is all you, nobody else. All the support crew is gone. It is hard to prepare for something like that. One way to do it is to attend a big event, especially if someone you know is fighting. Then you will get as close to the feeling as possible without being the one fighting. Of course, when it is you going into the ring, the feeling is much stronger, and you can't prepare for that. But by being at a big event as a corner or a training partner, you can get the closest simulation of what it will feel the first time you enter the ring.

If the pre-fight pressure builds and you can't control it, then it helps to do something to release it. Some people like to pace, others give a war cry, others like to hit the sparring pads. Regardless of your preference, once you release the extra tension, you can regain your focus. To develop a good routine you should look back at your matches and see what worked for you as mental preparation. Keep what is good and throw away what is bad, refining it with each fight. Once you develop a certain routine and it is successful, stay with it.

Regardless of which style of fighter you are, it is always a good idea to go over your plans for the fight, what you want to do in the first minute and so forth. Go over a few "what ifs" so that you can have a last review of the roadmap that you want to follow in this fight. There is no point in projecting too far into the fight, because who knows what will be happening beyond the first few minutes. By the middle of the fight you aren't thinking about anything except the moment. By then, I am emotionless. In my fight against Sakurai, he took me down and hit me in the head and I thought, "Damn, this is going to be a hard fight!" But I did not panic. The secret is to remain calm and not get exasperated. The calmer you are, the clearer you will think.

Everyone is going to get hit at some point. When you get hit, you can have two reactions. You can react by being scared, or you can react by hitting back. I am the second kind of person. When I get hit, I say to myself, "Oh man, I'm going to give it back to him!" You have to have that attitude. Sometimes it is good to train when you are tired, and have people pounding on you. Because then you get used to being in the worst possible situation. You develop a certain toughness.

Taped hands ready to rock, November 2004. Kid Peligro photo

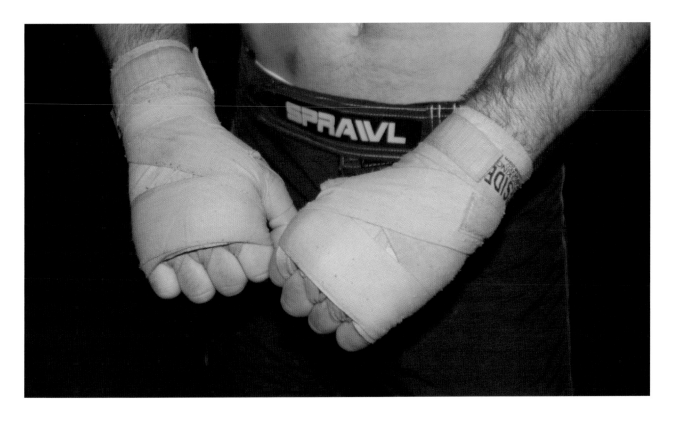

7

Of course, there will be times when you are so spent that you have nothing else to give. For one reason or another, you have used all your energies and you cannot hit back. Then it is your defensive skills and your heart that will get you through the fight and allow you not only to survive but to somehow reverse the fight and finish with a win.

That's right: even when you are totally spent, you must believe that you are going to win. You can't have any doubts. If you go into the ring knowing that you are not in your best physical shape, then you are adding a lot of extra pressure on yourself. Many times your toughest opponent is your

Rodrigo clears the leg and delivers a kick of his own against Takase. Pride Bushido, October 2003. Luca Atalla photo

own imagination. You always imagine the fight to be harder than it will ever be, and that motivates you to train hard, study your opponent well, and come prepared. It's a serious business that we are in.

For me to be able to concentrate and relax, I try to not put any pressure on myself. I tell myself I am going to win. Losing cannot cross your mind! Prior to my fights I come down to the hotel lobby with my crew and I start to listen to music. I especially like Eminem's song from the *8 Mile* soundtrack called "Lose Yourself," the part that goes, "Look, if you had one shot, or one opportunity, to seize everything you ever wanted—one moment—would you capture it or just let it slip?"

In my mind the message is, "Are you willing to risk everything for success?" If you had an opportunity and it was everything you wanted in life, would you take the risk? Would you take the chance? To be a successful fighter I believe you have to be ready to risk it all for the chance of achieving your dream! The bigger the risk, the greater the glory!

That is the choice we are faced with. Most people won't take that risk. They'd rather keep their savings. But there are those who want the big prize. That is why I fight against the top fighters and have never walked away from a tough fight. I know how I got here, and if I have to start over, I'll do it smiling, knowing that I tried, that I took the chance at the big prize.

This kind of mental frame is the key to success. If you worry about the risk, then you won't get in the ring with the confidence, the free mind necessary to win. That is what I live for. I don't hide behind anything. Once you achieve that mindset, there is nothing that can stop you! I want my enemies to feel fear when they hear my name. That is why I fight!

Conditioning

Your physical conditioning is closely related to your mental preparation. You should already be in reasonable shape before you take on the responsibility of a fight, but year-round shape is not fighting shape. You can't permanently maintain the kind of intense conditioning level that is required for a fight; you would end up burned out and injured all the time. The body needs rest, so the trick is to stay in reasonable physical condition all the time, but then to step it up to the next level at the right moment so that you peak during the week of your fight.

I have a training regimen that I like that involves increasing my cardio fitness, doing strength exercises to increase my power, and plyometric exercises to improve my explosiveness and reaction time. Bulking up helps improve strength at first, so in the early stages I do this and don't worry about conditioning. As I get closer to the fight, I taper down and start adding more cardio with the strength. As I get closer to a fight, I want to get leaner without losing strength. The goal is to get as agile and explosive as possible without losing strength. During the later phases of training, I use more interval training to increase my ability to perform during a fight. I might work out for one minute, then rest for one minute.

If you don't have a conditioning coach, you should get a good conditioning book for fighters. I recommend my cousin Royce's book *Superfit*. His training is very similar to mine.

As I said, you want your conditioning to peak about the same time as your fight, not a couple of weeks before or after. The most common mistake I see—especially with beginners, but sometimes even with veterans—is that their excitement and dedication cause them to train too hard, to peak too soon, and to be burnt out by the time the actual fight comes. It is important to pace yourself in preparation for a fight. Your body and mind both need to rest regularly in order to be sharp and ready to quickly react to the ever changing environment of hard sparring and competition. Regular rest also helps prevent injuries.

Too many people believe that they have to train to exhaustion every day. If you train to the point of exhaustion, after a short while you won't want to train anymore. The challenge is to keep pushing yourself, yet to always leave some energy in reserve, so your desire never leaves you. Of course, there are times and places where you have to push your limits in order to develop new skills and mental toughness. A good fighter will instinctively know those moments when they occur. But they don't occur every day!

One of the most important characteristics that a fighter has to have to be successful is discipline. You have to know when to get serious and train. When I sign up for a fight, everything stops. I do not talk to my wife or my kids. I train and think of nothing but the fight. Once the fight is over, then you can relax.

Sparring

Early in training I introduce the techniques I feel are necessary to add to my game or to refresh my game in order to best fight my opponent. I begin with repetition against a willing opponent who is lighter than me. Once I have the mechanics down, I start to increase my sparring partner's resistance incrementally. At this point I start to further understand what I need to work on to apply the techniques and get the timing right. Once

I have that down, then I use it in full technical sparring without strikes, with my partner fully resisting. At this point I begin to evaluate how comfortable I am with the technique and how my opponent reacts to it and tries to escape it. Then I see what options I have to counter his escapes.

To get a position down, you have to repeat it many times. Too many practitioners learn a position, repeat it a few times, and quickly want to use it in sparring. I suggest to my students that they repeat a position at least a hundred times before they try to use it. If you don't repeat and practice the position with a willing partner, you will never get the proper mechanics of the move. The next step is to repeat the move in training to develop the proper timing of the move. Once you have it down in training and sparring, then you can think about using it in a match. The worst thing is to try to use something you are not executing perfectly against an opponent that can strike you back. Then your mistakes and imperfections may cost you the fight! I recommend that you use a new move as a warm up, instead of spending ten minutes doing push-ups and sit-ups before training.

Only once I am totally comfortable with a move against a willing partner do I introduce striking and see how the techniques work under duress and how I can best apply them so that they are effective. This part is very important because you need to fully understand that NHB is not submission grappling, where your opponent cannot strike you. In NHB you have to always be mindful that there is a real possibility of your opponent nailing you

Teamwork! Trainer Martin Rooney gets Rodrigo ready to fight. Luca Atalla photo

while you attempt a submission or a reversal or any other technique. So at this stage of preparation I evaluate the dangers of the techniques and decide what angles I need to use to deny my opponent the proper opening for striking.

For example, if I do a triangle from the guard and I allow my opponent to reach proper posture, he may be able to rain down solid punches on my head, or he may be able to lift me and slam me down. So first I become aware of the negatives of each position and how I counter them. In the case of the triangle, I try to pull the opponent's head down to prevent him from reaching proper posture and having leverage to punch. Another option is to push his hips away with one of my legs so that he is stretched out and almost falling face down on the triangle. In the case of the slam, the quickest defense is to lasso your opponent's leg to prevent him from standing. If he stands, you have to let go of the triangle right away, otherwise a slam with the possibility of a knockout will follow.

This is therefore a critical stage of training. You may even have to discard some techniques that you have added because you cannot perform them safely. The important thing to remember here is that every situation and every technique applied by one person's body type against another's will yield different danger areas. (For example, if your opponent is short,

An experienced team greatly helps: Rodrigo taking last-minute instructions from Royce Gracie. Rumble on the Rock 6, November 2004. Kid Peligro photo

the slam from the triangle may not be as dangerous as it would be from a long-legged opponent.) Make sure you explore this stage and have your sparring partners be creative and look for angles and ways to strike you so that you can see the dangers and determine solutions and options to avoid them.

This technical training phase is also where I develop and finesse my moves that I like. As I get closer to the fight, I start to get away from the hard training and just concentrate on details and small adjustments. The week of the fight is not the time to train hard, because you want to avoid injuries. It is important, if you want to become a professional fighter, not to get injured before your fight and have to miss an event. I cannot overemphasize this. If you are frequently getting hurt before your fights, after a while the promoters will not seek you for their shows. So as you get closer to the fight, you need to train intelligently. Slow down the energy level of the sparring sessions, train only with partners that you know and trust, and cut down on the amount of outside training (such as conditioning), so that you accumulate all your energy for the fight. Don't leave your energy in the gym and come out flat! When fight time comes, you want to explode against your opponent.

Much like sport jiu-jitsu and submission grappling, The NHB game has an order and a hierarchy of positions. You should always progress in proper order and maintain the position you have achieved before you proceed to another one. This is imperative in NHB fights, since losing a good position may cost you the fight. When learning the techniques that I show, or in preparing for a match, do not be in a hurry. Go from position to position, with the first intent of maintaining what you've got, then advance to the next position until you are ready to submit your opponent. Remember, in a fight you spend a lot of energy achieving every little gain. If you are not tight and easily lose positions, you will tire more quickly. You will also become frustrated. Imagine the following: After spending minutes and a lot of energy passing the opponent's guard to side-control and finally achieving the mount, you allow him to escape with a bump and you end up on the bottom. You will have a sense of failure, and that is not a good feeling to have when your opponent is trying to beat you up!

Now let's look at another situation. You have steadily gained position, beginning in your opponent's guard. Despite his best efforts and struggles, you managed to advance to side-control. Once there, you kept him tight under you while occasionally delivering a strike or two to his head and ribs, just to remind him that you mean business. After controlling the position, you have achieved the mount. Your opponent has struggled, bridged, tried elbow escapes, everything, but you are still on top of him.

Just for good measure, you deliver a punch to his face. How do you think he feels? He is the one getting frustrated, he is the one losing control of his emotions, he is the one ready to quit, his spirit deflated and defeated while yours is just oozing with confidence! That is the way to fight; that is the way to win!

Your Team

You cannot train and progress alone. You need to have proper partners and coaches around you to help you achieve your goals, therefore selecting a proper team and a good school with experienced instructors is a must. The higher you aim your sights, the better the training and the coaching you will need, so be realistic and decide early on if you are in this just to be a better street fighter or to become a world champion. Your needs will be different depending on your final objective, but it is always best to look for a school that has good advanced students and coaches experienced in the fight game.

Ideally, your teacher will have direct fighting experience, or at least will have coached a few fighters in battle. It's helpful if your training partners have been in battles themselves, and can relay to you their experiences and what they've learned form their bouts. If you are surrounded by people who have no experience whatsoever, then your path is more difficult. You cannot rely on their advice as much, and won't get the chance to go to a top show as their corner man or second.

As you start to progress on your path, you will realize how important your team is. Your coaches will always be there to point out the areas where you need work and to correct any technical mistakes you are making. Your sparring partners will be able to give you different "feels" to mimic your opponent or to force you to develop certain parts of your game. For instance, if you are going to fight a very good wrestler and you expect to be on the bottom during the fight, you need to train with partners who are good at staying on top and passing the guard, so that they force you to develop your guard and strikes from the bottom.

Many times in my training I do specific positional training. If I am to fight a wrestler, I may have my partners stay in my guard and throw punches while I have to defend, try to submit them, or reverse the position. Other times I will have them on side-control and I have to escape. Once I escape, we start over. I also employ several partners so that I constantly must go against fresh fighters, because you have to know in your mind that you are capable of escaping a position no matter what, and no matter how tired you are.

Over time, you will develop a solid team and a camaraderie like no other. You and your teammates will not only trust each other, but they will understand how you react and which is the best option for you to execute at any given stage of the fight. Those are the people you want in your corner. My corner people keep me on pace and focused. You cannot have a person that gets so excited that they tell you to just go, go, go. If your corner man's advice is to just kick ass, then you need to look for someone else to be in your corner. What I look for in a corner man is for someone who knows my style and who gives me advice based on my preferences and what I do best. For instance, if I get in a good position and I have three options to submit the guy—a straight armlock, an omoplata, or a triangle—I want my corner man to know which I do best and to instruct me to get my body in a position for that option, rather than telling me to do what he likes best!

Developing a Fight Strategy

In the NHB world, it is very hard to remain on top for long. There are so many things that you need to know, so you almost always will find someone whose game matches up favorably against yours. It is easier for a boxer to remain on top for years, because the rules and possible approaches are limited in boxing. On any given day in NHB, anything may happen. So it is important for you to try to control the variables as much as possible, and

**The Guillotine is always there.
Pride Bushido, October 2003.**
Luca Atalla photo

you do that by learning the other facets of the game, like kick-boxing, Muay-Thai, and wrestling. If you fight against lesser opponents, you allow yourself some margin of error, but the higher you go up the ladder, the smaller the margin of error gets. The fight is sometimes won way ahead of entering the ring, by preparing correctly, having the right mental attitude, the proper strategy, and the right technical knowledge.

In fighting you need to have good technical skills for striking, closing the distance and clinching, takedowns, and ground techniques. You do not have to have an endless arsenal of strikes and clinches or takedowns, just learn the basics and have them down pat. The same thing goes for the ground game. Have enough solid techniques to be able to pass the guard and the half-guard, defend the guard and the half-guard, and to do reversals, sweeps, and submission techniques.

It is important for you not to try to learn everything at the same time. You have to specialize in something. My specialty is Gracie jiu-jitsu, and I also train in Muay Thai and wrestling to complement my game. If your background is boxing, you should be very good in boxing before you start to add anything else. I believe that Gracie jiu-jitsu is the best specialty for NHB. I firmly believe that unless you are exceptional at one discipline, you are not going to be successful in the fight game. What brings you victories and success in NHB is the ability to bring the game to your specialty. At the same time, you need to learn the other arts for three reasons: to counter your opponent's attacks, to learn how he thinks and reacts, and

A pre-fight routine will get you in the proper mental state to face your opponent and greatly increase your success: Rodrigo hitting the mitts. Luca Atalla photo

to have some surprises in your game. I don't practice kick-boxing with the intent to knock out my opponents, I practice it so I can learn the distance and timing of strikes, so I know when I'm at risk. Of course, if I fight against another fighter that has weak strikes, I will try to knock him out, or I may hit him enough so he wants to go to the ground—my realm.

You never know who you are going to fight against until one or two months prior to an event, so it pays to have a good broad skill base. But always, the goal is to take the opponent out of his comfort zone and into yours. If he has good strikes, I have to train in wrestling and takedowns, to bring the fight to the ground. If I fight a stand-up match, exchanging strikes, his chances of winning go up tremendously.

Conversely, if your specialty is striking and you are not good on the ground, then you need to train in takedown defense and basic counters to submissions, so that you can avoid the takedown and keep standing. And if you happen to end up on the ground, you will at least have the basics of submission defense so that you can survive and hope to get back up to your element. You learn jiu-jitsu to prepare for the worst, but your fight strategy is to be standing and trading strikes.

The Art of War is the perfect book to learn about fight strategy. It says that before you go into battle, you have to know yourself and you have to know your opponent. You have to know your strength and weaknesses, and you have to know your opponent's strengths and weaknesses. You will try to hide your weaknesses and take advantage of his, and he will do the same. The winner will be the fighter who prepares the best strategy.

Don't forget the element of surprise. When you do something that your opponent is not expecting, you may get a big advantage. For example, my cousin Renzo once fought Maurice Smith, a former Kick Boxing World Champion with a devastating array of kicks and punches. Renzo, of course, is a Gracie jiu-jitsu practitioner. The last thing anyone expected was for him to try to exchange punches or kicks with Smith. So what happens? Just as the fight begins, Renzo throws a leg kick to Smith's thighs, completely surprising Smith. Smith was momentarily confused, and that was all the advantage Renzo needed to take the fight to the ground, where he submitted Smith.

Another classic example is when my cousin Royce fought Hidehiko Yoshida in Pride Shockwave 2003. Royce is a Gracie jiu-jitsu specialist who had never fought without the gi. Yoshida is a former Olympic and World Judo Champion who can use the gi to his advantage. So Yoshida's training was based on the premise that Royce would wear the gi. When Royce took his gi off at the last minute, Yoshida's whole plan went out the window. Royce was able to control the entire fight.

If you know that your opponent is a better striker than you, and he knows that you want to take him to the ground, you might want to fake a takedown attempt, then strike him as he is reacting to the expected takedown move. The confusion from the unexpected move may linger for the entire fight, because from then on he won't know whether you are faking the throw for a strike or are really going for the throw, and that will open up the takedowns as well. Also, sometimes a striker may be so convinced you only want to take him down that he may even drop his guard, and that may be the opportunity to knock him out or to do some psychological damage.

People sometimes talk about a lucky punch that won a fight, but I don't believe that. When you take advantage of an opportunity, it is not luck, it is timing and execution that came from all those hours and months and years of training and strategizing and preparation!

The techniques I decide to emphasize for a particular fight depend on my opponent. I try to study tapes of his previous fights so I can determine his strengths and weaknesses. Then I design a strategy that takes advantage of his weaknesses and minimizes his chances to use his strengths. The first thing you need to do is to collect as much video of his fights as possible. Watch the fights and observe what he does well, what he doesn't do well, his preferences. Does he like to rush the opponent? Is he a counter-striker? Is he a good wrestler who doesn't like to go to the ground? All these things will help you greatly in achieving the proper strategy. I like to watch the tapes with my coaches and sparring partners, so we are all on the same page. Because they are your training partners, they will know what you like to do, and will be able to point out how you can take advantage of the opponent's tendencies. They will also be able to better mimic your opponent's game when they spar with you.

For instance, when I fought Takase, I watched some of his previous fights and I observed that he was a very flexible guy with a difficult guard. So I had my uncle Rillion, who is extremely flexible, come and help me train. I had him use the same style as Takase so that I could get used to the unorthodox approach.

It is also important for you to put yourself in your opponent's shoes. Watch your own fight tapes and analyze your own tendencies. See what he sees in you and try to think what his game plan to fight you will be. If he is smart, he is preparing for the fight much in the same way as you are. Seeing your own tendencies will tell you what he expects you to do against him. If you have always come out and kicked with the right leg, or always try a certain sweep, he is going to prepare for that, and with that info you can think of the next step to counter his counter. That is how you develop strategy.

One of the ways I open up my game is by watching top fighters. I have watched fighters like my cousins Royce, Rickson, and Renzo, and others like Wanderlei Silva, Quinton Jackson, and Rodrigo "Minotauro." I watch what they do in fights and I learn from it. By watching them fight I see what their vision is and how they react to things. I especially watch the difficult situations, because I want to learn about difficult situations before I get into them. Then I may put myself into that situation in training and see what I need to do to get out of it. I may even do what they do and see if their solution works for me, or if there is a way to adapt what they do for my game.

Teaching

When I have a student that wants to fight NHB, first I evaluate him. Where he is in training, what his strengths are, what he needs to develop. The next step is to see who is going to be his opponent. The next step is to formulate a general strategy to face that opponent, taking into consideration the amount of time we have to prepare and the ability of my student to absorb what I want him to learn. I may simply work on the elements he has that will work best against his opponent. If he has a good jab, I will incorporate that in the strategy and have him sharpen it up as much as possible.

Depending on the amount of time, we might not study anything new. If you don't have enough time to hone the new techniques in your student's game, you are doing him a disservice. It will just confuse his game. The new stuff will not be natural to him and will in effect be useless.

To be a great fighter, you need time and the proper environment to grow—technically, emotionally, and spiritually. You should plan your training and your fight progress, because if you fight an easy opponent when you are starting, you will be able to make mistakes and he won't necessarily capitalize on them, but if you fight a top-notch opponent, any mistake could be lethal, and that could hinder your development as a fighter.

In forming your training plan, make sure you take time into consideration. If you have time to prepare, then add one or two techniques at a time, and don't try anything else unfamiliar until they are absorbed into your game.

Another thing you can do is to improve your worse defects. It is easier to improve your worse characteristic by 20 percent than to improve your best characteristic 10 percent, so if your worst characteristic is important for the fight, you should dedicate some of your time to that and you will show a lot of improvement. If your worst characteristic can be hidden, then you should find the ways to do that, so it doesn't become a factor in the fight.

Another thing I try to do is to build on the techniques that are already there. If my student has a good position that he likes to use and has success with it, then I try to add another option from there, because his opponents will certainly know that he likes to do that and will have prepared a counter for it. Many of the techniques that I chose for this book are linked in that manner. If you get here and he does this, then you do the next technique. It is easier to build on a certain move than to give another completely detached move, because if the student is comfortable getting a certain sweep, or a certain technique, he will more likely feel at ease with another technique of the same family, rather than something on the opposite end of the spectrum. Neighboring techniques share a common approach and a common timing.

Even if I have to improve a certain area of the student's game that is not strong, I will still look for something he does well there and expand on that, because this way I don't have to force him to learn a whole new world. The instructor cannot simply teach the student what he himself

Rule #1 in NHB: Protect yourself first! Rodrigo controls Takase's legs before attempting the guard pass. Pride Bushido, October 2003. Luca Atalla photo

likes, because everyone is different. A good teacher will look at a student and improve what the student is naturally good at.

When you are using this book to improve your game, start with the techniques that are closer to your game. After you have mastered them, look to add the others, always going for the nearest technique to your preference and then progressing to the ones that are farthest from your comfort zone. If you find a certain technique that does not fit your style, even after you've tried and tried and talked to your instructor, then that may not be for you. But make sure you give these techniques a chance, because I chose techniques that encompass the entire game and that are adaptable to most biotypes.

Another thing you need to take into consideration when preparing someone to fight is at what technical level they are and what techniques they are ready to learn. You cannot take someone who has only one year of Gracie jiu-jitsu and teach him the most advanced positions because he simply will never get into a position where he can use the technique, and even if he gets to the position, he will not be able to execute it properly with the right timing, so it may be better to simplify his game than to try to give him an advanced weapon that he doesn't know how to use. It is like giving an M16 rifle to someone who never even used a handgun; it really won't help him, he'd be better off with a club than an M16. So evaluate your own place in training with a realistic eye and look for the technique that you can easily absorb first before going for the sophisticated ones. It is more important to add techniques that fit your understanding of the game.

Surprisingly, having a background in fighting is not that important. Many times it is easier to teach someone who knows nothing about martial arts than it is to get someone with some habits from one art and develop him into an NHB fighter. If you take a boxer and he is not used to being on the ground, it may be difficult for him to get comfortable there. Someone who knows a striking art is always thinking about striking. When you teach him to pass the guard, he keeps thinking about how to strike from there, not paying attention to the nuances of weight distribution and pressure that it takes to pass the guard. It is important, if you come from that type of background, to keep an open mind and concentrate on the ground techniques.

Of course, if you have a grappling background, it is easier to learn Gracie jiu-jitsu techniques for NHB. And a highly conditioned athlete has an easier time than a couch potato. But in general, the background doesn't make that much of a difference. If the student has an open mind and practices properly, he will achieve his goals.

Adjusting Grappling Techniques to NHB

Many sports jiu-jitsu and submission grappling techniques work well in NHB with little change, but some do not translate well. When considering a technique for NHB, two very basic and important questions should always come to mind. First, can I get hit from this position, and if so how do I protect myself? If there is not a good answer to that, then it may be better to avoid that technique altogether. Second, how can I hit my opponent from here? I stay away from fancy moves in NHB matches and just use the meat and potatoes. When you are fighting a sports jiu-jitsu match and there are no punches raining down on you, it's a lot easier to experiment with fancy moves. When you fight NHB, the first order of business is to protect yourself and not give your opponent a chance to knock you out. When your opponent is inside your guard striking you, you can't just ignore the punches and just go for an armlock.

It is important to always be looking to adapt the different techniques in Gracie jiu-jitsu and other fighting arts to NHB. If you go to a kick-boxing academy to learn strikes because you are going to fight NHB, they are going to show you punches and kicks, but those moves won't be ready-made for NHB. For instance, they may show you a certain high kick and say this is a good kick, but you know that if you use that high kick in an

Rodrigo controlling the hips with his tight passing game against Genki Sudo. 2001 ADCC.
Marcelo Alonso photo

22

NHB fight, especially against a wrestler, he is going to catch your leg and take you down. The first thing they teach boxers is to be in a sideways boxing stance, but if you fight NHB that way you expose your front leg to kicks, and you allow yourself to be taken down because your base is not there.

When transitioning from sports jiu-jitsu techniques to NHB techniques, one of the most important changes is to stop using your arms and hands to block the person on top from passing the guard. Every time you stretch your arms and use them to block the pass or to push the knee away, you leave your face open for strikes. One of the ways to learn to adapt your game is to practice with your partners and allow them to use light open-hand strikes, to make you aware of the dangers and to get you always thinking first of protecting yourself from a devastating strike. One of the specific trainings I do is to have the guy on top punching and me on the bottom defending and countering with submissions. When the guy is actually punching, things are very different. This will make you aware of the openings and the adjustments that need to be done. Sometimes it is a matter of increasing the speed of execution, other times it is a matter of actually protecting yourself and even allowing the opponent to advance to a position where he can't hit your face so easily.

In training your teammates have to replicate your opponent's moves: Rodrigo mounted and ready to apply the key-lock (technique 83) during fight preparation, November 2004.
Kid Peligro photo

Meet the Team

THE AUTHORS

Rodrigo Gracie

Rodrigo Gracie is the young lion of the Gracie clan, an international sensation since he burst on the scene in 2002 with a stunning victory in Pride, one of the most important events in the Ultimate Fighting world. The grandson of Brazilian jiu-jitsu founder Carlos Gracie, Rodrigo now has a string of victories at Pride and is one of the major draws in NHB, fighting before tens of thousands of spectators. With a nearly perfect record and with unlimited potential, Rodrigo is fast becoming the next superstar of Brazilian jiu-jitsu. He runs his own academy in Los Angeles.

Kid Peligro

One of the leading martial arts writers in the world, Kid Peligro is responsible for regular columns in *Bodyguard* and *Gracie Magazine,* as well as one of the most widely read Internet MMA news sites, *ADCC News.* He has been the author or coauthor of an unprecedented string of bestsellers in recent years, including *The Gracie Way, Brazilian Jiu-Jitsu: Theory and Technique, Brazilian Jiu-Jitsu Self-Defense Techniques, Brazilian Jiu-Jitsu Black Belt Techniques, Brazilian Jiu-Jitsu Submission Grappling Techniques,* and *Superfit.* A black belt in jiu-jitsu, Kid's broad involvement in the martial arts has led him to travel to the four corners of the Earth as an ambassador for the sport that changed his life. He makes his home in San Diego.

Phillipe Nover, *Assistant*

Phillipe is a purple belt under Rodrigo Gracie. He has been training for more than four years with Rodrigo, and has helped him prepare for many fights. He has a Muay Thai background, having done it for ten years. Phillipe won his first NHB match and is a promising fighter.

NHB Techniques

NHB matches can be divided into two types of fighting: stand-up and ground. Stand-up fighting includes kicks, punches, and elbow and knee strikes that occur while standing, along with clinching and takedowns. Ground fighting includes limited striking, along with reversals and submissions.

STAND-UP FIGHTING

For a jiu-jitsu or grappling practitioner, the stand-up part of the fight is perhaps the most dangerous. Since he is usually not as adept in that dimension, being able to avoid and block strikes is a must. Another important aspect of stand-up fighting is to be able to fend off clinches and takedown attempts, and to be able to execute your own.

While it is not in the scope of this book to teach you how to strike, Rodrigo shows you several practical uses for strikes, along with blocks and counters. Most important for any jiu-jitsu fighter wanting to succeed in NHB is the notion of distance and clinching. Strikes operate best at certain ranges. The ability to sense these ranges will help tremendously, not only in staying at a safe distance from strikes but also in effectively delivering strikes of your own and closing the distance to clinch, so you can safely execute takedowns.

Distance Drills

The notion of distance is extremely important for an NHB fighter. Being able to ascertain if you are too far to be reached by a punch, elbow, knee, or kick can be the difference between victory and a KO! If you don't know how close you have to be for your strikes to hit your opponent, then you will be wasting energy with your strike attempts and giving your opponent opportunities to counter and either strike back or clinch.

In NHB there are four distances or zones:

1 The safe zone: too far to be hit by a kick or too close to be hit by a knee or an elbow.

2 The kicking zone.

3 The punch zone.

4 The knee and elbow zone.

The safe zone can be divided into the far safe zone (fig. 1A) and the near safe zone (fig. 1B). The far safe zone is the closest that you can be to your opponent and still not be reached by a kick, punch, knee or elbow. This generally means you are far enough away from the opponent that his extended leg cannot reach you. The near safe zone is the space where you are so close to the opponent, most of the time at or near a clinch, that even close-up strikes such as the knees and elbows cannot do damage to you because there is not enough distance for them to develop power. Somewhere between the far and near safe zones lie the striking zones for kicks (fig. 2), punches (fig. 3), knees, and elbows (fig. 4). And one's ability to properly read these areas is of the utmost importance in a fight.

There are many exercises you can do to understand, learn to evaluate, and "see" these zones. Rodrigo prefers to use moving drills to achieve this. Below is one of his favorites. These drills involve using a partner and going through the entire gamut of strikes until you develop a sense for how far and how close you need to be for each of the zones.

1 Stand in front of your opponent with an orthodox stance (same foot forward). Have your opponent extend his arms, and then throw right and left straight punches or jabs. Start far enough away that you cannot be hit by the punches, and then slowly cut the distance until his punches can hit your face. At that point you may either bob and weave to duck his punches, or block them with your elbows as Rodrigo does here.

2 Start at the safe zone, and then get slightly closer to your partner until you can touch his shoulder with your extended hand. If you can do that, your knee will be able to reach his face when you pull him downward. Raise your knee and deliver a strike to his face. Next, have him execute the movement, striking your face.

3 Have your partner throw a straight punch, then cut it off with your elbow and pivot your feet in order to throw a punch with your back hand. This way you will develop the notion of distance for both the jab and the straight punch.

4 Standing in front of your opponent, throw some jabs and other punches. Start out at the safe zone and slowly close the distance until you begin to connect. Then retreat and approach again slowly.

5 Have your opponent throw a jab and follow with a shoot to your front leg. Block the punch with your left forearm and hand and block the shoot with your elbow.

6 Starting from the safe punch zone, throw a few punches. As you get closer, your opponent leans back just enough to avoid being hit. Continue throwing punches as you retreat and approach slowly in order to develop your sense of distance.

7 Stand close enough so that you can be hit with a kick, and have your partner throw a few light kicks to your front leg. Raise your knee to block the kicks. Move in and out of that zone.

8 Start by standing far enough away so that kicks cannot hit you, and have your partner throw a few kicks. Move in and out of that zone slowly as you learn to feel the different distances. If you get close enough that the kicks no longer work, you may be getting in the close-striking zone where elbows and knees are effective.

9 Start at the safe zone with your opponent throwing all the strikes slowly. Move in until you get to the clinch or the near safe zone. Stop at each of the zones and make mental notes to familiarize yourself with their boundaries.

10 With both hands on the back of his head, clinch your opponent and pull him in as you lift your knee for a knee strike. Do this several times, starting as far away as possible while still being able to reach the opponent. Slowly get closer, concentrating on both developing the motion and learning the knee strike distance. This drill can be done for elbow strikes as well.

Getting up in base

While submitting or knocking out your opponent is the ultimate objective of an NHB fighter, being able to survive a difficult situation is a must. In this case, Rodrigo is on the ground with the opponent standing, ready to take advantage of the situation. Rodrigo wants to protect himself and get back up.

1 Rodrigo is on the ground with Phillipe standing ready to deliver strikes. Rodrigo curls his legs toward his chest, grasping his shins with his hands (with the padded side of the gloves facing out), and pulls his legs up. Pulling the legs closer to the chest with the hands helps rest the legs and adds power to the strike. Notice how Rodrigo's toes are pointed up, with the bottom of the feet facing Phillipe, which adds another shield.

2 Rodrigo kicks out with his left leg, aiming at Phillipe's right knee. Rodrigo's objectives are to stop Phillipe from getting close enough to deliver a kick, and to force Phillipe back so that Rodrigo can get up. Rodrigo keeps in mind an imaginary line that is marked by Rodrigo's full leg extension. Since the line also represents the striking distance for Phillipe's kicks, it is a line that Phillipe cannot cross. Notice that in order for Phillipe to kick, he has to plant one of his legs first; that is the leg Rodrigo will strike to keep him from getting set to deliver an effective kick. Rodrigo may have to do this several times before the right opportunity to get up appears; until then Rodrigo will kick Phillipe's knees any time he gets inside the range of his extended leg. Jiu-jitsu is a game of patience; haste at this point will get you in trouble. Take your time and wait for the proper moment before you try to stand up.

3 Having created some sense of danger for Phillipe, Rodrigo is now able to prepare to stand. He sits up and turns his body to his right, planting his right hand back and his left foot on the ground next to his buttocks. Rodrigo coils his right leg, ready to deliver another strike to Phillipe if necessary, and uses his bent left arm at eye level to protect his face from strikes. Important: never get up as the opponent is moving forward, or he will have power in his strikes; always wait for him to react and move back before you get up.

4 Rodrigo demonstrates the proper base here, using his right hand and left foot as base points. Pushing off his right arm and left leg, Rodrigo lifts his hips off the ground and kicks out with his right leg, striking Phillipe's right leg. This strike has more power than the previous strikes, because Rodrigo gets his entire body behind the kick and forces Phillipe to retreat.

5 Rodrigo pulls his right leg back through the gap created by his right arm and left leg, and then plants his right foot slightly past his right hand. Notice that Rodrigo still keeps his left arm in front of his face throughout the entire motion to shield from strikes. Also notice how Rodrigo maintains his base at all times and ends up in a perfect three-point base.

6 Rodrigo gets back up, repositions his hands in a guarding stance, and is ready to fight. **Very important:** Notice that throughout the entire motion, Rodrigo keeps his eyes on Phillipe. At no time does he lower his eyes to the ground. It is extremely important to maintain eye contact with your opponent at all times; otherwise you will not see an attack initiation, and you will lose precious milliseconds before reacting to it.

Stand-up combination: jab to roundhouse

To be a complete and successful fighter, you have to have combinations, both in the stand-up game and on the ground. One of Rodrigo's favorite combos is the jab-roundhouse kick combination, because the jab draws the opponent's attention to his head, opening up the chance to land a low kick. If you only strike high or low, it will be easier for your opponent to focus his defense on that area. Mixing high and low attacks forces him to worry about his entire body. You set up your kicks with a punch. Normally you set up the straight right with the jab. That is what your opponent expects, but in this case you throw the jab and, instead of the punch, immediately follow with the kick. One of the major benefits of kicking is that you force the opponent to walk backwards.

1 Rodrigo and Phillipe stand in an orthodox stance, where both fighters have their left leg forward.

2 Rodrigo extends his left arm and throws a jab, forcing Phillipe to push off his front leg and lean back to avoid being hit. This position leaves Phillipe's front leg exposed to strikes.

40

3 Rodrigo pivots off the ball of his feet, squaring his hips forward.

4 Pushing off his back foot, Rodrigo swings his leg around to deliver a roundhouse (or side-kick) to Phillipe's left leg. Rodrigo aims for the back of the thigh, rather than a bony part of the leg such as the knee. Aiming for soft tissue not only inflicts the greatest damage to his opponent, but also minimizes the chance of Rodrigo hurting his own foot.

Stand-up combination: right cross to high clinch

Another great combination in NHB is the right cross to high clinch. Rodrigo fakes the clinch by flexing his knees and dropping his body down as if he is going for a low shoot. Don't exaggerate the drop; just do enough to get the opponent's attention. Rodrigo follows with a right cross, forcing the opponent to acknowledge the strike by either defending it or absorbing the punch. Rodrigo follows this with a clinch. If the opponent doesn't defend the punch, he will be hit and maybe knocked out. If he defends it, then he can be clinched.

1 Rodrigo and Phillipe face each other. Rodrigo bends his legs and drops his body, bringing Phillipe's attention to the lower part of his body.

2 Pushing off his back leg, Rodrigo loops a right cross over Phillipe's guard, striking him in the face.

3 Rodrigo takes advantage of the attack by taking a big step forward with his right foot. He makes sure that his right knee moves past Phillipe's left knee, and he slides his right hand under Phillipe's left armpit in order to lock his right arm around Phillipe's body. Note how important it is that Rodrigo's right leg is very close to Phillipe's left leg; otherwise he will not be able to maintain control when he clinches.

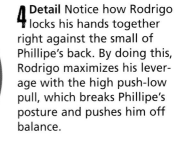

4 Rodrigo reaches with his left hand around Phillipe's torso until he can lock his hands together. Rodrigo cinches the clinch by bringing his chest and head tight against Phillipe's chest. Rodrigo then forces Phillipe's lower back towards Rodrigo's hips by pulling his his own arms in while driving his head forward. This motion forces Phillipe's chest back and causes Phillipe to lose his base. One final motion pushes Phillipe off base: Rodrigo drives his right thigh (and knee) against Phillipe's left leg, causing it to buckle slightly. Notice that this takedown movement is not straight back, but rather pivoting the drop over Rodrigo's right thigh.

4 Detail Notice how Rodrigo locks his hands together right against the small of Phillipe's back. By doing this, Rodrigo maximizes his leverage with the high push-low pull, which breaks Phillipe's posture and pushes him off balance.

5 Rodrigo continues with the push-pull motion as he pushes off his left leg and forces Phillipe to fall.

6 Rodrigo follows Phillipe to the mat, ending up in side-control position. Notice Rodrigo's controlling position: his hips are tight against Phillipe's hips, and his left knee is deep under Phillipe's left leg, which further removes any space for Phillipe to escape Rodrigo's hips. Rodrigo's left elbow presses against Phillipe's right hip, and his right arm is under Phillipe's left arm, thereby controlling the top of Phillipe's body.

Stand-up combination: left jab, straight right, high clinch

One can never have too many combinations; the ability to link together techniques will always lead to your opponent falling further and further behind in his reactions. Another one of Rodrigo's favorite combos is the left jab, straight right, high clinch. By bringing Phillipe's attention to the series of high strikes, Rodrigo opens up the clinch.

1 Rodrigo extends his left arm and delivers a left jab. This forces Phillipe to block by raising his arms, thus leaving the middle of his guard open.

2 Rodrigo immediately follows the opening created by Phillipe's reaction by pivoting his feet and pushing off his back leg to deliver a straight right punch that strikes Phillipe's face.

3 Taking advantage of Phillipe's attention to the high punches, Rodrigo steps forward with his right leg and plants his foot just behind Phillipe's left foot. He then wraps his arms around Phillipe's torso for the high clinch. From here, Rodrigo can use the same motion as in the previous clinch to bring Phillipe to the ground.

Stand-up combination: left jab, straight right, low clinch

A great variation of the previous technique is the left jab, straight right, low clinch. Using the same attack as before, Rodrigo diverts Phillipe's attention to the high punches and takes advantage of the reaction to clinch low for the double-leg takedown.

1 Rodrigo extends his left arm and delivers a left jab. This forces Phillipe to block the jab by opening his right arm, which leaves the middle of his guard open.

2 Rodrigo immediately follows the opening created by Phillipe's reaction by pivoting his feet and pushing off his back leg to deliver a straight right punch that strikes Phillipe's face.

3 Taking advantage of Phillipe's attention to the high punches, Rodrigo steps forward with his right leg and plants his right foot just behind Phillipe's left foot. At the same time, Rodrigo drops his body and wraps his hands behind Phillipe's knees for the low clinch. This sets up the double-leg takedown. Notice that Rodrigo's hands grip directly behind Phillipe's knee as Rodrigo brings his chest and head tight against Phillipe's chest. This maximizes his leverage for the takedown. Once again, Rodrigo drives his right thigh and knee against Phillipe's left leg. This forces Phillipe's leg to buckle slightly, which knocks Phillipe off base.

Stand-up combination: right cross to low clinch

Another very effective combination is the right cross to low clinch. Once again, Rodrigo uses diversion to create an opportunity for an attack. In this case he fakes going to a clinch. When his opponent reacts, he launches a right cross and then goes back to the clinch and takedown.

1 Rodrigo stands in an open stance facing Phillipe. Notice that Phillipe is in a south-paw stance, with his right leg forward; Rodrigo is in an orthodox stance, with his left leg forward.

2 Rodrigo bends his legs and drops his body as if he were going for a low clinch. This forces Phillipe to react, and he drops his arms to prepare to block the clinch.

3 Taking advantage of Phillipe's lowered hand guard, Rodrigo pushes off his back leg and launches a right cross to Phillipe's face. In this case, he strikes him on the chin; alternately, Phillipe might raise his hands to block the punch.

4 In either case, Rodrigo takes advantage of Phillipe's reaction. Here, the strike causes Phillipe to lose an instant of reaction time when Rodrigo steps forward with his right leg and clinches Phillipe. Rodrigo grabs Phillipe's left leg—with his right hand behind the left knee and his left hand behind the right calf—to keep Phillipe from kicking the right leg back. At the same time, Rodrigo drives his chest into Phillipe's mid-section while his head pushes against the outside of Phillipe's right side. His head placement is important, because Rodrigo would leave himself open for a guillotine choke if he pushed his head against Phillipe's chest instead. Even if Phillipe were able to apply the guillotine, Rodrigo could still do the takedown by pushing Phillipe's torso to one side with his head while throwing his legs out to the opposite side. In this way, he would end up in side-control, and not in the guard where the guillotine would be more effective. Notice Rodrigo's wide base as he steps in with his right foot between Phillipe's legs, placing it near Phillipe's right foot in such a way that his own hips are square with Phillipe's front leg.

5 Rodrigo initiates the takedown by driving his right shoulder down and lifting Phillipe's right leg with his left arm. He also pushes his head toward his own right, which forces Phillipe's body to lean in that same direction. This pushes Phillipe off balance, as he falls to his left.

Stand-up combination: opponent jabs to clinch

No one is certain who will take the first step or throw the first punch during a fight. What you have to be sure of is that, regardless of who initiates the action, you have an option to deal with the situation. In this case, Phillipe throws a left jab and Rodrigo blocks and follows with a clinch on the same side. Notice that since the strike has been blocked with a parry, that side is the preferred side to come into for the clinch, because there is no immediate danger of a second punch.

1 Rodrigo and Phillipe face each other.

2 Phillipe launches a left jab. Rodrigo ducks his head to the right to avoid the punch; he also deflects the punch by swatting his right hand to the left. When blocking punches and kicks, it is important to use the least possible amount of action with the blocking limb, as you want to be ready to block another punch. Should you exaggerate on the motion—in this case by swinging the right arm hard to the left—you will leave an opening, because it would take a lot longer for your hand to get back in the protection mode.

3 Rodrigo steps forward and clinches Phillipe. Rodrigo grasps Phillipe's right thigh with his left hand and Phillipe's left calf with his right hand. Since Rodrigo already moved his head to the right, to avoid the jab, it makes it easy for Rodrigo to come in with his head on the right side of Phillipe's torso. Notice Rodrigo's feet and hip position in relation to Phillipe's legs. His hips are square with the front leg and his front foot is placed between Phillipe's legs near his back foot. Again Rodrigo makes sure he presses his head against Phillipe's left side to prevent him from attempting a guillotine.

4 With his left leg, Rodrigo takes a step to his left and initiates the takedown. He forces Phillipe off balance (to Phillipe's right) as Rodrigo drives his head against Phillipe's chest and pushes, while lifting Phillipe's left leg with his right arm.

Stand-up combination: jab counter to trip

Another great option when an opponent launches a high punch is to drop down to a trip. Since the opponent has just delivered a jab, he leaves his front leg and the same side of his body open to a clinch. Note that there is an element of danger when executing this type of a lunge, as the opponent can follow the jab with a knee strike from the back leg. Timing and execution are of the utmost importance. Make sure your outside hand blocks any possible knee strikes and your head is aimed to the outside of the opponent's front leg as you lunge forward. You have to be fast! Should your head come in centered, it will be right in the power range of the knee strike. The more your opponent moves forward, throwing punches and kicks, the easier it will be to take him down. Always avoid walking back in a straight line, as you become an easy target for strikes. You have to constantly move away from his power hand. You can take one step back and the next to the side, or you can come in for the clinch.

1 Rodrigo and Phillipe face each other.

2 Phillipe launches a series of left jabs. Every time he comes in to jab, his weight goes on his front leg; this is the perfect time for Rodrigo to come in, because Phillipe cannot shift his weight to his back leg for the knee strike. Rodrigo ducks his head to the right to avoid the punch, at the same time deflecting. As before, he flicks his right hand to the left to swat the punch away.

3 Rodrigo moves from the deflection into a clinch. He drops his body deep down as he takes a step forward with his left/front leg and bends his knees. He also squares his hips forward and pushes off his back leg to initiate the lunge.

4 Pivoting on his left foot, Rodrigo drops his left knee down to the mat and lunges forward, clinching Phillipe. Notice that Rodrigo grabs the back of Phillipe's knees with his hands, making sure his torso is erect and his head is up; he is pushing tight against Phillipe's body. It is important for Rodrigo to connect with Phillipe before dropping the knee to the ground. In this way, he can execute the movement in a controlled manner and not hurt his knee.

5 Detail In this close-up of Rodrigo's right leg trapping Phillipe's left ankle, note that the toes of Rodrigo's right foot point out, and the top of his foot faces down.

5 Rodrigo circles his right leg around Phillipe's left leg, hooking Phillipe's heel and trapping his ankle with Rodrigo's calf. At this point Phillipe cannot move his left leg.

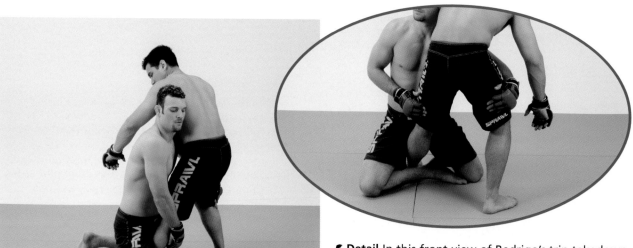

6 Detail In this front view of Rodrigo's trip takedown, Rodrigo drives his hips against Phillipe's left knee. This forces the knee to Rodrigo's right as he pulls his own right leg back to trip Phillipe. Notice that Phillipe falls to Rodrigo's right, and not straight back, as the pressure on the knee moves in that direction.

6 As he continues with his forward momentum, Rodrigo takes down Phillipe by pressing his own hips to his right, against Phillipe's left knee. He makes sure to maintain the lock on Phillipe's left ankle.

7 As Phillipe's back hits the mat, Rodrigo executes a figure-four around Phillipe's left ankle by locking his right foot behind his own left knee. Rodrigo applies a knee bar by driving his hips down on Phillipe's left knee and lifting Phillipe's legs with the figure-four lock. He pulls Phillipe's ankle up, hyperextending the knee joint.

8 In this side view, notice Rodrigo's figure-four lock around Phillipe's left ankle, and the position of his right calf as it is pressed against Phillipe's heel. Rodrigo's right foot is locked behind his own left knee. Rodrigo executes the knee lock by straightening his legs as he pushes his hips forward and down against Phillipe's knee.

Stand-up combination: right-cross counter to hip throw

One of Rodrigo's favorite counters to a right cross is the hip throw. Once again, Rodrigo takes advantage of the opponent's action and counters it with a take-down, taking the fight to his element, the ground. In this case, Rodrigo uses a hip throw. The hip throw is a powerful throw when executed well, as the opponent is launched high over the attacker's back. Rodrigo finishes the move with an armlock from the knee-on-stomach position.

1 Rodrigo and Phillipe face each other.

2 Phillipe shoots his right arm out, throwing a right cross. Since the cross has a curve in it, Rodrigo blocks it by circling his left hand toward his ear. By bending his arm at the elbow, Rodrigo can protect the entire right side of his face. The blocking arm motion is similar to the motion of running your fingers through your hair. When you try this motion, remember to twist your body slightly away from the punch while stepping in slightly, because another punch may be coming.

3 Rodrigo immediately wraps his left arm around Phillipe's right arm, locking his arm under Phillipe's armpit while stepping forward with his left foot.

4 Rodrigo takes a looping step with his right leg, placing his right foot past Phillipe's left foot, and pressing his hips against Phillipe's hips. Rodrigo makes sure his hips are square with Phillipe's body. Notice Rodrigo's right hand gripping Phillipe's right hip while his left hand grips Phillipe's right elbow. Also note his base, with feet opened slightly wider than shoulder width, and legs slightly bent.

5 Rodrigo steps around Phillipe's left leg with his right leg planting his right foot in front of Phillipe's right foot. At the same time, he squares his hips in front of Phillipe's. Rodrigo then bends his knees and drops his body further, locking his hips with Phillipe's hips. He executes the hip throw by extending his legs and lowering his head toward the mat. He also pulls Phillipe's right arm with his left hand, and Phillipe's hips with his right hand, rotating Phillipe's body as he throws him over his hips down to the ground. A few tips for when you begin this movement: first, begin by placing your feet square in front of your opponent's feet; you should be able to draw a square between the four feet. Also, it is important for your hips to edge out slightly beyond your opponent's hips for more control. Your legs should be at shoulder width; otherwise your opponent might fall on and hurt your leg.

6 As Phillipe hits the ground, Rodrigo plants his right knee on Phillipe's stomach while maintaining control of Phillipe's right arm. He then executes a figure-four lock around Phillipe's elbow by reaching with his left hand over his own right wrist and placing his right hand on Phillipe's right shoulder. Rodrigo applies the armlock by thrusting his hips forward while arching his torso back to apply pressure to the elbow joint.

Stand-up combination: roundhouse kick counter to takedown

Today's NHB fighters not only know how to punch, but also are very adept at kicking. The low side-kicks and roundhouse kicks to the thighs or the side of the torso are commonly used to slow the opponent down and undermine his stamina. If not countered properly, the thigh kick eventually renders the leg useless, forcing a fighter to fall down during the match, while the kick to the side may break ribs or cause the fighter to lose his breath. It is important for you not only to learn how to deliver kicks but also how to block them and take advantage of the block in an effective manner. In this case, Rodrigo shows a common block to the thigh kick and a takedown from the block.

1 Rodrigo and Phillipe face each other.

Point the knee out.

2 Pivoting on his front foot, Phillipe throws a right roundhouse kick to Rodrigo's left leg. Since the roundhouse has a long arc to travel before it reaches its target, Rodrigo is able to intercept it by taking a step forward with his left leg, making sure he points his knee towards Phillipe's shin. It is possible that Phillipe's kick may hit Rodrigo's knee, but with the proper angle, shown here, the kick should deflect up and Rodrigo will be able to trap it. Notice that timing here is extremely important; should Rodrigo fail to initiate the counter step as soon as Phillipe begins his kick, he will not be able to intercept the kick before it reaches its power range.

3 Rodrigo catches Phillipe's right leg and wraps his left arm around it. This allows him to secure control of the leg by trapping it between his arm and body.

4 While keeping Phillipe's leg up in the air, Rodrigo takes a step forward with his right leg and hooks it behind Phillipe's left leg. This movement trips Phillipe at the same time it knocks him off balance, because Rodrigo is also pushing with his right hand against Phillipe's right shoulder. Notice that the path of Rodrigo's right foot is like that of a figure eight; he first kicks the foot forward between Phillipe's legs and then kicks the heel back for the inside trip.

5 Phillipe falls to the mat while Rodrigo keeps control over his right leg. Rodrigo ends up with his right foot planted on the ground near Phillipe's hips between the legs. At this point Rodrigo has a wide array of options, including a footlock, a knee bar, or strikes.

Stand-up combination: high-kick counter to straight punch

Kicks to the head are devastating if they connect, but they are also a great risk for the kicker, since he compromises so much of his balance. Still, many NHB fighters have them in their arsenal and like to use them. If the kick connects, the benefits are great; but even if the opponent blocks, there are still many opportunities to clinch and execute a takedown or throw a direct punch, as Rodrigo does here.

1 Rodrigo and Phillipe face each other.

2 With his right leg, Phillipe delivers a high kick to Rodrigo's head. Rodrigo blocks with his left arm by making a semi-circle with his hand, as if he were trying to punch a target next to his ear. Notice that Rodrigo's blocking arm motion follows the same pattern as if he were running his fingers through his hair. At the same time, he twists his body slightly to the right and leans back away from the strike. This minimizes the strike's full impact, absorbing its power. When you try this move, don't try to catch the strike; always worry about blocking first!

3 Having blocked the kick, Rodrigo takes a short step out with his left leg and wraps his left arm around Phillipe's right heel so that he can trap the heel under his armpit. Notice that Rodrigo traps Phillipe's leg between his arm and his torso, and cinches the hold by pressing his left hand against his own ribs.

4 While still controlling Phillipe's right leg, Rodrigo pushes off his right leg and throws a straight right-hand strike to Phillipe's face. Notice that Rodrigo could execute a takedown, as he did in the previous technique, instead of the punch.

Takedown counter: sprawl to guillotine

The ability to foil takedowns can never be underestimated in NHB. Ideally you want to be able to decide when, if, and how the fight goes to the ground. Perhaps you are fighting an opponent that has a very good top game, like a wrestler who would like nothing more than to take you down and be in your guard, delivering punches (called the ground-and-pound technique). Being able to effectively defend takedown attempts is a must, but even better is to have options for attacks from the blocks. Rodrigo would normally use the common sprawl technique, but this time he was slightly late and follows with a guillotine choke. Notice that the guillotine is an option that is almost always available when a clinch is taking place. If you are the one doing the clinch, be sure to be looking for it and have a defense at the ready. If you are the one defending the clinch, remember that you can use this effective attack just about every time.

1 Rodrigo and Phillipe face each other.

2 Phillipe shoots forward, clinching Rodrigo by grabbing the back of Rodrigo's knees with his hands. To counter the takedown attempt, Rodrigo turns his hips toward Phillipe and drives the hips forward and down as he sprawls. Unfortunately, the sprawl attempt is late, and Rodrigo realizes that he is going to be taken down.

3 Realizing that he only partially blocked the takedown, and that he is ultimately going down, Rodrigo looks for the guillotine. He leans forward with his torso and moves his right arm to circle Phillipe's head.

4 Rodrigo applies the lock by sliding his right arm under Phillipe's head, with the blade of his forearm pressing against Phillipe's throat. Rodrigo wraps his left arm around Phillipe's right arm until he is able to grab his own right wrist with his left hand. This helps him apply the upward choking motion of the guillotine. Notice how Rodrigo drapes his chest over Phillipe's back to help his arm reach around Phillipe's neck. At this point, Phillipe is still proceeding with his takedown attempt and Rodrigo is starting to fall back.

5 As he falls, Rodrigo makes sure he escapes his hips to his left and opens his right leg, leading Phillipe to fall inside his guard. Notice how Rodrigo's right leg is extended out to corral Phillipe's body into the guard. Also, Rodrigo is already applying the choking pressure by pulling his right wrist up with his left hand. Keep in mind that the guillotine choke pressure works with the blade of the forearm pressing up against the throat—not pulling up toward the head. Think of the motion of a window as it goes up in its track; that is the motion the forearm should mimic for the proper guillotine choke.

6 Having trapped Phillipe between his legs, Rodrigo closes his guard by locking his left foot over his right one. This traps Phillipe's torso inside the guard.

6 **Reverse view** This reverse view clearly shows Rodrigo's left arm around Phillipe's arm.

Stand-up single/double leg counter: sprawl to footlock

The single and double leg takedowns are very common clinching attacks in NHB matches. In the single leg, the fighter lunges, grabbing the opponent's leg and pulling it for the takedown. In the double, the attacker grabs behind both knees and pulls them for the takedown. Because these are such common attacks, there are many counters to them, the most common being the sprawl. In this technique, Rodrigo demonstrates the counter and reverses Phillipe, completing the move with a footlock.

1 Phillipe lunges forward, taking a big step with his left leg and shooting to grab Rodrigo's right (forward) leg. Rodrigo immediately counters by placing both hands on Phillipe's shoulder, using his left forearm to block and to keep Phillipe away. As Rodrigo sprawls, he springs his feet back while driving his hips forward. At this point, Rodrigo could try to deliver a few knee strikes to Phillipe's head, depending on how balanced and in control he feels at this moment.

2 Rodrigo continues the counter, as he further sprawls, by stepping back with his right leg. With both hands, Rodrigo pushes down on Phillipe's head, towards Phillipe's right side, forcing him facedown on the mat. Notice how Rodrigo drives the weight of his body, with his chest pushing down on Phillipe's back to keep him down. Meanwhile, Rodrigo's left hand continues to push down on Phillipe's neck, to keep it pinned to the mat.

3 Once he has Phillipe's face against the mat, Rodrigo quickly changes the control. His right hand leaves Phillipe's back, and circles around his head and under his throat, locking his hand on the right side of Phillipe's chin. He then pulls it to the left, while his left hand goes from Phillipe's neck to grabbing his right triceps. Notice that Rodrigo keeps pushing his body weight down on Phillipe's left shoulder. His right shoulder is preventing Phillipe from standing back up. Rodrigo also uses his left hand to pull Phillipe's right elbow open, preventing him from opening the arm and bracing it to help himself get up. Both moves also further force Phillipe's head to the mat.

4 Rodrigo circles to his left, around Phillipe's head. He brings his right knee in, and steps around with his left leg, as he assists the motion by pulling on Phillipe's right arm with his left arm. Notice that Rodrigo is really close to Phillipe's right leg at this point.

5 Rodrigo reaches with his left hand, and grabs Phillipe's right calf to pull it up. He also drives his head against Phillipe's hips, forcing Phillipe to roll over his shoulders, and putting Phillipe's back on the mat. Notice that during the entire motion, Rodrigo is circling to his left. At this point, Rodrigo could simply release the grip and be satisfied; he has executed the takedown, and has achieved side-control on Phillipe.

6 Rodrigo plants his right hand on the mat, and steps with his left foot over Phillipe's left leg. He pushes down on Phillipe's right leg, with his left hand driving it towards the mat, across Phillipe's body.

Right knee keeps Phillipe down.

7 Rodrigo leans back, and slides his right knee forward, while looping his right foot and hooking it between Phillipe's legs. This prevents Phillipe from coming up to defend the footlock.

8 Rodrigo circles Phillipe's right ankle with his left arm, and applies the footlock by arching back, and extending the foot while driving the hips up. Notice that Rodrigo loops his left leg all the way around Phillipe's right leg, putting his left foot against Phillipe's stomach. This prevents Phillipe from sitting up to counter the pressure.

Stand-up strike: knee

NHB is a game of takedowns, submissions, and strikes. If you neglect any of these areas, you severely limit yourself and your options. And once your opponents realize your shortcomings, they will take advantage of them, making it more difficult for you to reach the situations you prefer in a match. The next few moves demonstrate a series of strike counters and combinations. First is a knee strike as a follow-up to a blocked punch.

1 Phillipe and Rodrigo are facing each other, and Phillipe throws a left jab-right punch combination. Rodrigo blocks the jab by closing both forearms in front of his face, and then he blocks the right punch by bringing his right hand to the back of his head. This movement mimics the action of combing his hair. As he pivots off his feet, Rodrigo turns his torso to his right.

2 When Phillipe drops his hand, and starts to pull the arm back to regain his hand posture, Rodrigo pivots off his feet again. He turns his hips so that he is facing Phillipe, reaches with his right hand, and grabs Phillipe's right shoulder.

3 With his right hand, Rodrigo pulls Phillipe's shoulder forward, and then propels his right knee up to Phillipe's face. Notice how Rodrigo reaches full extension of the strike, for maximum power, by pushing off the left foot until only the ball and the toes are on the ground.

Low-clinch defense to kick

The shoot for a low clinch is one of the most common takedown attempts in NHB. If successful, the opponent will secure your leg, pull you down to the mat, and be in good position to pass the guard. One of the best ways to counter the shoot is by blocking the shoot with the elbow and following it with a kick. After a few unsuccessful attempts, followed by this type of punishment, your opponent will think twice before he tries to take you down again, and that hesitation and fear will work to your advantage.

1 Phillipe and Rodrigo are facing each other. Phillipe throws a left jab, and follows it with a low shoot. Rodrigo drops his body down, bending at the knees, while keeping his torso semi-upright. He blocks the shoot with his left forearm and elbow, hitting the left side of Phillipe's neck. Notice that to get low, Rodrigo doesn't bend at the waist, while keeping his legs straight, but rather drops down, bending the knees while keeping his torso at a 45-degree angle for best power.

2 While keeping the forearm block against Phillipe's neck, Rodrigo takes a big step back and around to his right with his left leg and steps in with the right foot . He also pulls Phillipe's head and neck down with his left hand. Rodrigo uses his right forearm to press down on Phillipe's left shoulder, forcing him to the mat. Phillipe either opens his arms and braces the fall, or he falls face-down on the mat.

3 Pushing off his arms, Rodrigo extends his torso back and around to his right, as he brings his left leg forward, kicking Phillipe's face. Notice that Rodrigo uses the push of his arms to propel his body around, creating the circular momentum for the kick.

Low-clinch defense: evasion

At times your reaction to the shoot may be late and you cannot drop down fast enough to use the previous technique and block with your forearm. In that case, all is not lost, as Rodrigo demonstrates here.

1 Phillipe and Rodrigo are facing each other. Phillipe throws a left jab, and follows it with a low shoot. Rodrigo has not reacted quickly enough to drop down and block the shoot with his elbow and forearm, and so Phillipe is able to reach with his left arm between Rodrigo's legs, and attempt to grab Rodrigo's left leg.

2 Rodrigo quickly steps out and around to his left with the left leg, as Phillipe falls to the mat.

Straight jab to double-leg takedown

One of the best ways to clinch an opponent is to follow a strike. The opponent generally reacts to a strike by leaning back to avoid it, rendering him vulnerable to the clinch. Even if he were to throw a counter strike of his own, his momentum is going the wrong way and his strike won't have any power behind it. In this case, Rodrigo throws a straight left jab and follows it with a low shoot for a double-leg takedown.

1 Rodrigo and Phillipe are facing each other. Rodrigo takes a short step with his left leg as he drops down and throws a left jab, forcing Phillipe to lean back to avoid getting hit. With Phillipe leaning back, it is the perfect moment for Rodrigo to shoot in.

2 Rodrigo shoots in as he leans forward, dropping his left knee to the mat between Phillipe's legs, as he encircles the legs with his arms. Rodrigo's hands aim to grab the back of Phillipe's knees. Rodrigo continues his forward motion, as he takes a big step with his right leg so that his right foot lands past Phillipe's legs. He springs his torso up, driving his head just behind Phillipe's left armpit. Notice that Rodrigo drives his chest into Phillipe's body, forcing him back and off balance. It is important for Rodrigo to step with the right leg, and for his right foot to land beyond Phillipe's body. In this way, he pushes Phillipe off balance as he drives his body into Phillipe's waist.

3 Rodrigo stands up, taking a big step out to the left with his left leg, as he lifts Phillipe's left leg with his right arm. At the same time, he drives his torso to his left and pushes his head against Phillipe's left side, forcing Phillipe to fall. Notice that since Rodrigo lifts Phillipe's left leg, all of Phillipe's weight now is on his right leg, making it easier for Rodrigo to take him down to that side. Rodrigo continues to push Phillipe to the right and pulls Phillipe's right leg from under him, forcing him to fall to the mat with Rodrigo ending up in side-control.

Punch counter to knee strike

Whenever your opponent throws a strike, your first thought should be to avoid or block it. Only after you have accomplished one of these options should you consider a counter-attack. In this case, Phillipe throws a right cross and would follow with a left punch. Rodrigo blocks the first punch, makes sure he controls the second, and only then comes back with a knee to the belly.

1 Phillipe and Rodrigo are facing each other. Phillipe initiates the action by throwing a right cross. Rodrigo steps in with the left foot, and intercepts it with his extended left arm, making sure he cups his hand behind Phillipe's right triceps, to keep him from pulling back. Phillipe then attempts a left cross, and Rodrigo immediately intercepts it with his right arm. Notice that because Rodrigo has cut the distance between himself and Phillipe, the second punch does not have much space to develop, making it easier for Rodrigo to intercept. Rodrigo cups his right hand behind Phillipe's left arm, to prevent him from pulling it back and throwing another punch.

2 Rodrigo steps around to Phillipe's back as he loops his right hand under Phillipe's left arm. He clinches by reaching around Phillipe's back, locking his right hand on Phillipe's right ribcage.

Pull the arm to clear a path to the belly.

3 Pushing off his left leg and pulling Phillipe forward with his arms, Rodrigo delivers a knee strike to the belly. At this point Rodrigo can continue and use the next technique (19) for a takedown as well.

Punch counter to takedown

A very good option from the punch counter shown in technique 18 is to go for a takedown. If you are the type of fighter who likes to take the fight to the ground right away, this trip takedown will do the job.

1 Phillipe and Rodrigo are facing each other. Phillipe initiates the action by throwing a right cross. Rodrigo steps in with his left foot and intercepts the right cross with his extended left arm. He makes sure to cup his hand behind Phillipe's right triceps, to keep him from pulling back. Phillipe then attempts a left cross, and Rodrigo immediately intercepts it with his right arm.

2 Rodrigo wants to regain control of the center, so he pummels with his arms. First, he circles his right arm inside and under Phillipe's left arm, until he locks his hand behind Phillipe's neck. Then, he follows the same pattern with his left arm inside Phillipe's right. Once he locks both hands behind Phillipe's head, Rodrigo pulls Phillipe's head down.

2 Detail Notice how Rodrigo grips the back of Phillipe's neck, with his right hand pulling on Phillipe's head, and his left hand placed behind the right one. His elbows are closed together, trapping Phillipe's head and preventing him from pulling his head out.

3 Rodrigo takes a big step back with his left leg, as he pulls Phillipe's head down even further. This forces Phillipe to follow him. He shoots the left knee up, delivering a knee strike to the head. Notice that Rodrigo not only shoots the knee up, but also pulls Phillipe's head into the strike, all the while pivoting off the arm pull to add power to the strike.

Takedown counter: sprawl to knee strike

One of the best ways to counter a shooting takedown is to sprawl. By shooting your feet back and pushing your hips down, you deflect the shooter's power and ability to control your hips and legs. Rodrigo goes one step further with his sprawl, forcing Phillipe to the mat and delivering a little punishment with a knee strike to the head.

1 Rodrigo and Phillipe face each other. Phillipe drops down, bending at the knees, and shoots low, aiming at Rodrigo's legs.

2 As soon as he sees Phillipe shooting low for his legs, Rodrigo defends the takedown attempt with a deep sprawl. He shoots his legs back, while driving his hips down, which forces Phillipe to fail in his attempt to gain control over Rodrigo's legs. Notice that since Phillipe shot low, Rodrigo was able to drop the weight of his chest on top of Phillipe's back, while at the same time pushing down on Phillipe's head with his left hand, forcing him face-down on the mat.

2 **Reverse angle** Notice how Rodrigo sprawled. Since his left leg was in front, Rodrigo pivoted off his right foot and shot his left leg back, while twisting his hips to his left. This breaks any chance of Phillipe's securing a grip on that leg. Also notice how Rodrigo uses his left hand to push down on the back of Phillipe's neck, forcing his head to the mat, and how he pushes off his toes to force his chest against Phillipe's back.

3 While pressing down with his chest on Phillipe's back, to prevent him from standing, Rodrigo brings his right knee to the mat next to Phillipe's head, and wraps his left arm around Phillipe's neck, grabbing the left side of the jaw with his hand.

Raise hips high for greater power.

4 Rodrigo lifts his left leg up, with the heel pointing straight up, and cocks it to bring it down, striking Phillipe on the head. In some events, knees to the head may be illegal; in that case, Rodrigo may change to a guillotine, or simply spin around to Phillipe's side or back.

Clinch to knee strike to takedown

In a fight there will be times when you and your opponent are in a virtual stalemate. One very common case is the clinch shown here, where you and your opponent have similar control. At times like these, in close quarters, knees can be an effective option, so be aware of the possibility, prepare for the defense, and be ready to deliver your own strike. If Phillipe reacts to the strikes by closing the distance between their hips, Rodrigo will take him down with a trip.

1 Rodrigo and Phillipe are clinched, each with one arm under the other's armpit, and one arm over his arm. This is a virtual stalemate, and an extremely common position in stand-up fighting.

2 Rodrigo leans to his left and drops his left shoulder, while moving his hips back. This creates space between his legs and Phillipe's body.

3 Rodrigo slides his left forearm in front of Phillipe's hips, in order to block him from closing the distance, and to protect from any knee strikes that Phillipe may throw. Rodrigo then takes a short step back with his left leg, and brings his knee into the space where his left arm was, for a strike of his own.

3 Reverse angle Notice how Rodrigo reaches with his left arm, so that his hand clears all the way past Phillipe's left hip.

4 After the first or second knee strike, Phillipe will not allow Rodrigo to get distance. He reacts by bringing his hips in, and keeping his body straight.

5 Rodrigo takes advantage of Phillipe's reaction, and grabs him around the waist, over Phillipe's right arm. Rodrigo then steps forward with his left leg, so that his foot traps Phillipe's right foot. As he moves forward, he forces Phillipe to fall to the mat. Notice that Rodrigo twists his body to his left after he grabs Phillipe's torso, which is what forces him to fall; Phillipe can't step back with his right foot.

Clinch to knee strike (opposite side)

Another option to deal with the clinch is presented here. The clinch is so common that fighters spend a great deal of time pummeling and fighting for control in it, so different opportunities for attacks will appear.

1 Rodrigo has his left hand in front of Phillipe's hip, blocking him from closing the gap or delivering a knee.

2 Phillipe has Rodrigo's right arm trapped, with his left arm wrapped tightly around Phillipe's arm. Rodrigo reaches up with his left hand, grabs Phillipe's left hand, and pushes it down, releasing Phillipe's control over his own right arm, and pulls the right arm back as he steps back with his right leg.

3 Rodrigo leans to his left, forcing Phillipe's left hand down even further with his own left hand, and creating the space to pull his right hand out, as he takes a very short step back with the right foot. He makes sure to stay on the tips of his toes, in preparation for the strike. Rodrigo places his right hand on the back of Phillipe's neck, and pulls it down. At the same time, he brings the right knee up for the strike.

Clinch to arm drag to trip

Another option from the clinch is to go for this takedown. Rodrigo begins pummeling and quickly gets control of Phillipe's arm as he goes for an arm drag. Should Phillipe not react, Rodrigo will simply continue towards Phillipe's back. If Phillipe reacts properly by leaning back, Rodrigo changes and attacks with the trip, taking advantage of Phillipe's weight going back.

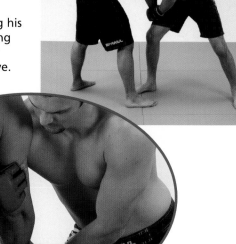

1 Rodrigo and Phillipe are in a clinch, with Rodrigo blocking Phillipe's hips in order to prevent the knee strikes.

2 Rodrigo slides his left arm back, so that his hand grips Phillipe's right wrist. Rodrigo pushes Phillipe's wrist down, and quickly pulls his right arm from under Phillipe's left arm. He will use his right hand to grab Phillipe's right elbow, as if he were going for the arm drag. Phillipe reacts to the arm drag by pulling his body back. He leans back, pushing off his feet so he can prevent Rodrigo from executing the move.

2 Detail Notice Rodrigo's grip for the arm drag. His left hand drives Phillipe's wrist back and outside Rodrigo's right leg, while the right hand pulls Phillipe's right arm by the triceps. The direction of the pull is down, inside, and forward at the same time.

3 Taking advantage of Phillipe's reaction of leaning back, Rodrigo drops his body forward. He steps inside Phillipe's legs with his right leg, and hooks Phillipe's right leg with his leg, trapping Phillipe's ankle with the nook of his knee. Notice that Rodrigo doesn't let go of his right-hand grip on Phillipe's right elbow, and he pulls Phillipe's torso down by the elbow.

4 Rodrigo's forward projection, along with driving his chest against Phillipe's right knee and sweeping back Phillipe's right foot with the right leg, forces Phillipe to fall back. Notice that Phillipe cannot step back with his right leg and regain balance, because his right ankle is trapped by Rodrigo's right leg. Rodrigo ends up on top of Phillipe, with his right leg trapped in Phillipe's half-guard, and with his right arm hooked under Phillipe's left arm.

5 Rodrigo raises his hips and uses his left hand to push down on Phillipe's right leg as he tries to free his right knee.

6 Rodrigo then brings his left foot back, and hooks it inside Phillipe's right leg at the knee. Rodrigo leans forward, and drives his right knee through the gap of Phillipe's legs. He then pulls up on Phillipe's right arm to force his back to remain flat on the ground. If Rodrigo allows Phillipe to turn to his own right, this maneuver won't work. Rodrigo continues to drive his right knee inside his left leg, until his foot hooks over Phillipe's right leg. At this point, he can open his left leg out, and exchange hooks from the left to the right foot.

6 Detail Notice how Rodrigo hooks his left foot inside Phillipe's right leg. The top of his foot pushes against the back of Phillipe's thigh, as close to the knee as possible.

7 Rodrigo ends up in side-control, as he finishes driving his right leg forward and releases the hook over Phillipe's right leg. One of the biggest keys to this pass is for Rodrigo to control Phillipe's upper body, and to force his back flat on the mat. For that he uses his hook on the right side. His chest drives forward, pressing Phillipe's chest flat. Rodrigo also pulls Phillipe's right arm up with his left arm, further flattening Phillipe to the mat.

Clinch attack: inside control to takedown

Some of the best ways to gain control in the clinch are to pummel faster and reach inside-control of the opponent's torso, or to test his balance by pushing, pulling, and twisting his torso. In this clinch exchange, Rodrigo tries to pull Phillipe forward by the right arm. Should Phillipe not react, Rodrigo will apply either a hip throw or a simple trip to the right leg and take Phillipe down. Phillipe counters by stepping around with the left leg and Rodrigo immediately changes for the inside trip.

1 Rodrigo and Phillipe are in a clinch. Rodrigo's right hand is under Phillipe's left arm, and his left arm is over Phillipe's right arm, with the hand gripping his elbow. Rodrigo's head is to the right of Phillipe's head. Rodrigo initiates the action by turning his chest to his left, and pulling Phillipe by the right arm. At the same time, he leans back on his left leg.

2 **Reverse angle** Rodrigo leans to his left as he pulls Phillipe's right arm with his left hand. This twists Phillipe in a counter-clockwise direction. Phillipe counters by stepping out with his left leg so that he can center his body with Rodrigo as he leans back. Rodrigo's right leg is now inside Phillipe's legs.

3 Rodrigo continues to lean, pulling Phillipe to the left, and further forces Phillipe's reaction. Rodrigo takes advantage of this reaction, as he bends at the knees, pivots his body to the left, and steps in with his right leg, hooking it behind Phillipe's left leg. Notice the motion as Rodrigo turns to the left and steps between Phillipe's legs with his right leg. Notice the direction of Rodrigo's right leg: his toes are firmly planted on the ground, with his heel pointing up. The knee points towards his left.

4 Rodrigo follows Phillipe's momentum going back to his right (clockwise), and drives his entire body in that direction. As he drops his torso down, his right arm drops to Phillipe's left thigh. Rodrigo uses his chest to push against Phillipe's stomach, forcing him off balance. Phillipe cannot step back with his left leg to regain his balance, and he falls to the mat with Rodrigo inside the guard.

4 Detail Notice Rodrigo's right leg, which is hooking Phillipe's left leg. Rodrigo's knee is on the ground, with its nook tight against Phillipe's ankle. Also, note that Rodrigo's right thigh pushes inside of Phillipe's leg, while his calf pushes on the outside, locking the leg and preventing Phillipe from raising it to step out.

Clinching after a jab

As previously stated, one of the best moments to clinch is following a strike. This works both ways: you can try clinching not only after you strike, but after deflecting or avoiding your opponent's strikes. Here, Rodrigo dodges Phillipe's jab and goes for the rear clinch.

1 Rodrigo and Phillipe face each other.

2 Phillipe throws a left jab, and Rodrigo counters by bobbing his head to his right, and deflecting the jab with a right-hand swipe. Notice that Rodrigo doesn't rely on just one, but both the head bob and the hand swipe to avoid the jab. He does this to make sure he doesn't get hit, and also to open the path for the rear clinch.

3 Rodrigo takes a step forward with his left leg, so that his foot lands right in front of Phillipe's left foot. As he closes the distance between himself and Phillipe, he drives his chest against Phillipe's back, with his arms open and surrounding Phillipe's body. Notice how Rodrigo's head is tight against Phillipe's left shoulder. He does that for two reasons: first, he wants to keep Phillipe from bringing his left arm around and in front of Rodrigo's face, negating the clinch; and second, it keeps him from being hit by Phillipe's left elbow strike, should he try one.

4 Rodrigo completes the rear clinch by locking his hands together, and stepping around Phillipe's back with his right leg. Notice how Rodrigo keeps his torso and head tight against Phillipe's torso for control. Also notice Rodrigo's leg position in relation to Phillipe's: he is not completely square on his back, but slightly off to the side, in order to keep control and balance.

Counter to the rear clinch: Kimura

A very common counter to the rear clinch is the Kimura. The Kimura is generally applied on the arm that is in front, clinching. The key to this counter is to be able to pry the opponent's hands apart and bring him to the ground into the guard so you can fully execute the Kimura. You may attempt to crank the opponent's arm around to his ear without placing him in the guard, but if you don't have complete control he may be able to walk around and counter, or simply go with the movement and circle around to avoid the submission pressure.

1 Phillipe has a rear clinch on Rodrigo. He is on Rodrigo's right side, with his right arm around Rodrigo. Rodrigo will attack that arm. First he needs to break Phillipe's lock with his hands clasped together, so he begins by grabbing Phillipe's right wrist with his left hand and driving it out. This opens the space for his right arm to wrap around Phillipe's right arm. Notice that Rodrigo's right hand must come in above Phillipe's right elbow, in order to lock the elbow and have the proper hold for the Kimura.

2 Once he locks his right hand onto his left wrist, completing the Kimura lock around Phillipe's right arm, Rodrigo steps forward with his left leg. He cranks the Kimura, driving Phillipe's arm in a clockwise direction, to break the hand grip. Rodrigo then cocks his right leg, bringing the heel up, and places his shin in front of Phillipe's hips. He hooks his right foot outside Phillipe's hips to the left.

2 Reverse angle (detail) Notice how Rodrigo has cocked his right leg, using the shin in front of Phillipe's hips to keep distance. He has looped the foot until it hooks outside of Phillipe's left hip, to prevent him from circling to Rodrigo's back. This also makes him end up inside the guard as Rodrigo goes to the mat.

3 Rodrigo hops to his left on his left foot, so he squares his hips and faces Phillipe. Rodrigo's right leg naturally turns and ends up on the outside of Phillipe's left hip. He then bends his left knee until his back is on the mat. Because Rodrigo's right foot was hooked on the outside of Phillipe's left hip, and his left leg is slightly outside of Phillipe's right leg, Phillipe ends up between Rodrigo's legs in the guard. Notice that as he does this move, Rodrigo is already torquing Phillipe's arm.

4 Rodrigo slides his body out to his left and turns onto his right side, always keeping his left leg on Phillipe's back, thus preventing him from rolling forward and over his right shoulder to escape the shoulder lock. Rodrigo's right leg position, with the heel locked against Phillipe's left thigh, prevents him from circling up to reach Rodrigo's side and to avoid the Kimura.

Kimura defense from the rear clinch

The previous technique demonstrated the Kimura as a counter to the rear clinch. This is a dangerous attack that needs to be dealt with properly, otherwise you risk the chance of being submitted. Rodrigo shows one way to counter the attack.

1 Rodrigo has Phillipe in a rear clinch. He is on Phillipe's left side, and his left arm is in front.

2 Phillipe applies the Kimura by first using his right hand to grab Rodrigo's left wrist, pushing it out and opening the space for his left arm to wrap around Rodrigo's arm. He reaches until his left hand can grab his right wrist, locking the Kimura around Rodrigo's left arm. If Rodrigo does not counter, Phillipe would attempt to crank the Kimura, twisting Rodrigo's arm in a counterclockwise direction.

3 Rodrigo quickly steps to his left to defend the arm, and to be able to lock his hands together again, gaining a few seconds to apply the counter. If Rodrigo simply stops here, Phillipe might have the leverage to break Rodrigo's hand grip again, and go for the Kimura.

3 Detail Notice how Rodrigo locks his hands again, with the hands in the form of a hook and the fingers (in a claw position) working together.

4 Rodrigo wraps his left leg around Phillipe's left leg, below the knee, and pulls it back, pushing and pivoting his right foot. He then drives his chest forward, forcing Phillipe to fall to the ground on his left side.

5 Once on the ground, Phillipe no longer has the submission. Rodrigo can release his hands as he plants his left one on the ground, which helps him to prop his body on top of Phillipe's back. Rodrigo hooks his right arm around Phillipe's right arm, grabbing his wrist with his hand. He then loops his right leg around, locking it inside Phillipe's right thigh for the hook, and securing the back. At this point, Rodrigo can either apply strikes to the back of Phillipe's head, or pursue a submission.

6 Rodrigo bends his left arm, dropping to his elbow as he pulls Phillipe over with him by the right arm. Notice how Rodrigo's left hand is already in place for the choke. Rodrigo then wraps his left arm around Phillipe's neck, making sure his elbow is centered with Phillipe's Adam's apple. His hand touches Phillipe's right shoulder, and locks the rear naked choke by grabbing Phillipe's right biceps with his left hand. Rodrigo also drives his right hand behind Phillipe's head. Rodrigo applies the choke by bringing his elbows together as he expands his chest and pulls his arms tight, as if he were hugging a longtime friend.

Takedown from the clinch: trip

A very effective takedown from the clinch is the trip. Although it appears simple, the trip, when properly set up, works surprisingly well. In this case, Rodrigo sets up the trip by trying to grab Phillipe's near leg, forcing him to pull it back and change his base, which leaves him vulnerable to the trip.

1 Rodrigo and Phillipe are in a clinch, with Rodrigo blocking Phillipe's hips with his left arm.

2 Rodrigo drops his torso down, and reaches with his left hand, trying to grab Phillipe's near leg (in this case the right one). Phillipe counters the grab attempt by stepping back with his right leg. Notice that at this point, Phillipe has changed his base by switching the forward leg.

3 Rodrigo shifts his weight to his right leg, as he bends it and leans to that side, while at the same time reaching with his right arm, up and under Phillipe's left armpit. He drives the torso to his left, as he pulls down and around on Phillipe's right arm with his left hand. Notice that Rodrigo's motion resembles the motion of turning a big wheel in a counterclockwise direction. This motion forces Phillipe's trunk to twist, and he becomes off balance as his right leg is not forward, in the proper place to brace and counter the motion.

4 Phillipe needs to step forward with his right foot to regain balance as his weight is going from his left to his right as Rodrigo pulls and twists him off balance. Rodrigo continues the twisting motion as he stretches his left leg so that his left foot blocks Phillipe's right foot when he tries to step forward to trip him. Phillipe cannot help but fall to the ground, and Rodrigo ends up in side-control.

4 **Reverse angle** Notice that as Rodrigo trips Phillipe, he continues to pull Phillipe's right arm around with his left hand, and he drives his right arm, which is hooked under Phillipe's left armpit, up and around. This actually pushes Phillipe forward, adding to the tripping motion.

Single-leg takedown counter to knee bar

The single-leg takedown comes up a lot in NHB. Knowing how to defend it is vital to success. Rodrigo shows an effective counter to the single-leg and advances to a submission.

1 Phillipe has Rodrigo's right leg in a single-leg grip, readying for the takedown. Rodrigo maintains his balance, hopping on his left leg, but he cannot stay there forever, or Phillipe will be successful and take him to the mat.

2 Rodrigo hops to his left as he pushes Phillipe's face away with both hands and hooks the right foot behind Phillipe's right thigh to counter the takedown. Pushing on the left side of Phillipe's face creates space for Rodrigo to free his leg slightly from Phillipe's control.

3 Rodrigo continues to push Phillipe's face away with both arms. Phillipe starts to lose control over Rodrigo's leg, and Rodrigo hooks his right arm inside Phillipe's left arm, near the armpit. He also holds his own right thigh with his right hand, thereby trapping Phillipe's left arm. Rodrigo leans forward with his torso, and plants his left hand on the mat for a brace.

4 Rodrigo shoots his left leg back out behind Phillipe, as he drops his body to the ground. At the same time, he hooks his left arm around the back of Phillipe's left ankle. Rodrigo scissors his legs, kicking his right leg back at the same time, and shoots his left leg forward, with his knee bent and his thigh hitting behind Phillipe's left ankle. Rodrigo also pulls Phillipe's left ankle forward with his left arm. This combination sends Phillipe falling to the ground, as Rodrigo prepares to lock his legs around Phillipe's left leg, trapping it for the knee bar.

5 Rodrigo locks his legs in a figure-four around Phillipe's left leg, with his right leg locked over his left foot. He wraps both arms around Phillipe's calf. Rodrigo applies the knee bar by arching back with his torso, while driving his hips forward against Phillipe's knee.

GROUND FIGHTING

This is the jiu-jitsu fighter's domain. Ground fighting typically is divided into fighting from the bottom (guard and half-guard) and fighting from the top (passing the guard, side-control, knee-on-stomach, mount, and back mount). The guard allows you to fight bigger opponents from a seeming disadvantage, even launching submissions and reversals from the position.

Fighting from the top generally involves a more aggressive posture than fighting from the bottom, with the exception of passing the guard, when one has to be extra cautious not to fall prey to submissions and reversal attempts. Unlike jiu-jitsu, where you have to rely on subtle submission attacks to create openings for moves, in NHB you can use strikes to create chaos and induce opportunities from your opponent's reactions to achieve positional gain or a submission and expose weaknesses in your opponent's defense. Rodrigo demonstrates strikes in many of his techniques. Even when he doesn't demonstrate strikes from certain positions, the possibility may be there. As you become comfortable with the positions, make mental notes and expand the techniques shown here.

GROUND FIGHTING

Closed Guard

Being able to fight with your back on the ground (in the guard) is an advantage of Gracie jiu-jitsu that was demonstrated to the world by my cousin Royce in his UFC matches. The guard is a great equalizer, taking away much of the weight advantage that a heavier fighter has over a lighter fighter. In NHB, the closed guard is a place where you have to maintain close control over your opponent's head so you can control the space between his torso and your face, taking away the distance necessary for him to effectively deliver punches. Once you have protected your face from strikes, the closed guard offers a variety of attacks and reversals.

Guard attack: closed-guard cross-sweep

Many times while in the closed guard you can take advantage of the opponent's attempts to escape the control. In this case, Rodrigo pulls down on Phillipe's head, breaking his posture forward. Phillipe counters by planting his hands on the mat and pushing back so he can lean back and regain proper posture to pass the guard or to strike. Rodrigo exaggerates the pressure, and when Phillipe overcommits, he applies the cross-sweep. The key here is to fight with the opponent for the control and surprise him with a quick release and take advantage of his momentum.

1 Rodrigo has Phillipe in his closed guard, and he uses his right hand to pull down on Phillipe's head. At the same time, he uses his left hand to pull on Phillipe's right arm, trying to break Phillipe's posture. Phillipe fights back by planting both hands on the mat, and pushing back to pry his head from Rodrigo's control.

2 Rodrigo quickly releases his grip on Phillipe's head, and uses Phillipe's backward momentum. Rodrigo releases his closed feet, opens the guard, pushes off his right foot, and sits up. At the same time, he reaches with his right arm across Phillipe's torso. At times Rodrigo can use this motion to deliver an elbow strike to Phillipe's face as he drives the arm across. Notice that as long as Phillipe is pushing off his arms, he cannot punch; as soon as he reaches back, and lifts his head, he can punch. Therefore, Rodrigo has to act quickly.

3 Rodrigo plants his left hand back on the mat, wraps his right arm around Phillipe's right arm, and pulls it in. At the same time, he pushes off his right leg, and drives his hips up and to his left, bumping Phillipe off balance. It is important that Rodrigo's hips are touching Phillipe's hips, to maximize the forward thrust.

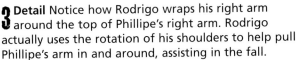

3 Detail Notice how Rodrigo wraps his right arm around the top of Phillipe's right arm. Rodrigo actually uses the rotation of his shoulders to help pull Phillipe's arm in and around, assisting in the fall.

4 Rodrigo continues the motion, forcing Phillipe to fall to the mat. Pushing off his left arm, Rodrigo takes a step over Phillipe's legs, landing on the left. Notice that Rodrigo places his left leg flat on the mat so that it doesn't obstruct Phillipe's fall. It is a common mistake to have both legs bent, with the knees pointing up, while attempting the bump. With this mistake, the knee will actually interfere and block Phillipe from falling.

5 Rodrigo continues to push off his left arm, and ends up mounted on Phillipe. Notice that Rodrigo did not try to come over the top of Phillipe, but actually rolled him to the side over his right leg. It is very important not to try to roll over the opponent, as his feet will prevent you from executing the movement. Instead, roll him over to the side, in a circular motion. Also, note that it is very important to sit up, to properly execute this movement. It is another common mistake to try to apply this sweep with the back slightly off the ground, instead of sitting up.

Guard attack: closed-guard cross-sweep to Kimura

A common counter to the cross-sweep is for the opponent to open his hand and block the sweep by bracing off the arm. In that case, you simply take advantage of him posting his arm up and go for a Kimura. We pick up from technique 38, step 3.

1 Rodrigo attempts to execute the cross-sweep, but Phillipe blocks it by moving his right hand out and posting his right arm.

2 Rodrigo uses his left hand, the one he was pushing off of, and grabs Phillipe's right wrist. It is very important for Rodrigo to control Phillipe's right wrist, before he does any other move. Otherwise, Phillipe will simply pull his arm out, and avoid any attacks. Rodrigo starts to let his back go down to the mat, as he brings his right hand to his left wrist, locking the figure-four with his arms around Phillipe's right arm.

3 Rodrigo rotates his shoulders to the right. As his back returns to the mat, Rodrigo slides his hips out to his left, driving Phillipe's right wrist up.

4 Rodrigo continues to slide his hips to the left, as he loops his left leg over Phillipe's back, to prevent him from rolling forward over his right shoulder and escaping the pressure. Rodrigo continues to torque Phillipe's arm around the shoulder, by pushing his right wrist toward his right ear in a circular motion.

4 Reverse angle Notice how Rodrigo has his entire torso out to the left, and his left leg draped over Phillipe's back. Rodrigo applies pressure on Phillipe's shoulder, by turning his shoulders to his right as he drives Phillipe's right arm around. Rodrigo has to be on his right side, and Phillipe's chest needs to be on the ground. Rodrigo's elbow must be behind Phillipe's shoulder, pressing down against it, so Phillipe can't stretch the arm.

4 Incorrect Phillipe is able to stretch and straighten his arm, because Rodrigo did not press Phillipe's right shoulder with his right elbow during the entire movement. It is very important to apply pressure with the elbow; otherwise, Phillipe will be able to adjust and straighten his arm.

Guard attack: closed-guard cross-sweep to guillotine

A third option for the cross-sweep is when the opponent not only blocks the sweep by planting the arm out but blocks the Kimura attempt by moving his torso forward. In that case, he exposes the neck for a guillotine choke. Remember, these options occur every time when you try the cross-sweep. You should be successful with the sweep, or your opponent will give you the Kimura or the neck for the guillotine. Practice them together until they become automatic and you will be surprised how effective they will become in your arsenal.

1 Rodrigo has Phillipe in his closed guard, and is reacting to Phillipe's posting to free his head and get posture. Rodrigo goes for a cross-sweep. This time, however, Phillipe leans forward with his body, pressing against Rodrigo's chest, and leading with his head.

2 Rodrigo circles Phillipe's head with his right arm.

3 Pushing off his right foot, Rodrigo slides his hips back to create space so that he can lock the guillotine. To execute it, he must reach all the way around with his right hand, until his left hand can grab (see detail). Notice that since Phillipe has his arm posted forward, Rodrigo's left arm had to go around the outside of Phillipe's right arm, and under the armpit. It is very important that Rodrigo scoot his hips back; otherwise, he would not find enough space to get his arm around Phillipe's neck. His chest would be too close to Phillipe's chest.

3 Detail Notice Rodrigo's handgrip. The right hand has the thumb pointing up, so that the blade of the forearm presses against Phillipe's throat. Rodrigo's left hand grabs under his right hand, gripping around the bottom of the hand.

4 Having locked the guillotine choke, Rodrigo starts to apply pressure by leaning back to the mat.

5 Rodrigo applies the finishing pressure by turning his body to his left as his back hits the mat. He pulls his right forearm onto Phillipe's throat, while pulling Phillipe with his legs. One important detail is that Rodrigo pulls his right hand up and in, as if he wants to touch his right shoulder. In this motion, he closes his arm around Phillipe's neck. Rodrigo lifts his left elbow up, as if he is turning a steering wheel.

Guard attack: opponent defends guillotine

Since the guillotine option is always available from the clinch, and it is a common attack from the closed guard, a veteran opponent will be alert to the attack and immediately counter it. In this case, Phillipe defends the guillotine, using his left hand to block Rodrigo's right hand from coming around the neck and locking onto his right hand, or, if the hands have already interlocked, pulling down on the wrist to release some of the pressure. Instead of fighting against Phillipe's defense, Rodrigo continues to another technique: he goes for a cervical hold and a sweep. We pick up the technique with Phillipe already in Rodrigo's guard, defending the guillotine.

1 Rodrigo attempts to lock a guillotine choke on Phillipe, but Phillipe counters it with his left hand, blocking Rodrigo's right hand from wrapping around his neck and locking onto the left hand.

2 Sensing the counter, Rodrigo slides his right hand under Phillipe's left armpit and drives his right arm through. He then wraps it around Phillipe's shoulder, making sure the palm of his hand faces up. Rodrigo drives his right arm up, as if he is reaching for an object above Phillipe's left shoulder. At the same time, Rodrigo releases his left arm, which was around Phillipe's right arm.

3 Rodrigo brings his left arm behind Phillipe's back, locking the palms of his hands together. Again, note that Rodrigo's right palm is facing up. Notice how Phillipe's head is trapped under Rodrigo's armpit, between the triceps and the upper ribcage.

3 **Alternate view** From this angle, notice how Rodrigo's hips are positioned to his left, and how he closes his left elbow in order to press down against Phillipe's right arm. This prevents Phillipe from bringing his right arm around and using it to punch. Rodrigo applies pressure to the back of Phillipe's head for the cervical hold. Often an opponent will submit just from that pressure.

4 Should the opponent resist, or turn his body to his right to reduce the pressure of the hold, Rodrigo will execute a sweep by stretching his legs as he drives his right arm up. The added pressure on Phillipe's neck will force him to roll to his right.

5 Rodrigo adds power to the sweep by opening the guard and hooking his right foot under Phillipe's left leg. From here, he can use it like an elevator, pushing Phillipe's left leg up and over.

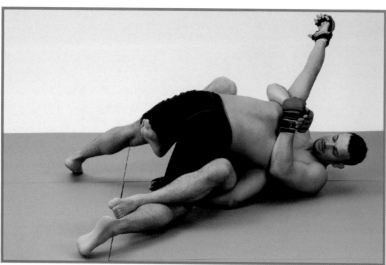

5 **Reverse view** Notice how Rodrigo uses his right foot hook, and how he uses his left foot to trap Phillipe's right leg. This keeps him from jumping over to the side.

6 Rodrigo lands on top of Phillipe, still locked onto Phillipe's neck.

7 Once he completes the sweep, Rodrigo loops his right leg around Phillipe's left leg for the mount. Rodrigo locks his feet under Phillipe's legs, securing the position.

7 **Reverse view** Notice how Rodrigo locks his feet under Phillipe's legs and pushes his hips forward, achieving complete control over the mount.

8 To finish the cervical lock, Rodrigo places his left elbow on the ground. He knows he must have his opponent's back flat on the ground, so Rodrigo uses his chest to push Phillipe's right shoulder to the mat. Should Phillipe be able to turn sideways, he will be able to reduce the pressure Rodrigo can apply.

9 Since Phillipe is very flexible, another option is to clamp his hands together and pull Phillipe's left shoulder toward the right, where his shoulder doesn't have the same range.

Guard attack: arm bar

In the previous technique Rodrigo was able to counter Phillipe's defense to the guillotine by going to the cervical hold and sweep. Sometimes, however, a wise opponent will counter that by planting his hands on the ground and freeing his head from the trap, stopping the cervical hold. In that case, go right for the arm bar. The key for these techniques to work is, as stated before, to have them ready to spring into action in an instant. By knowing the available counters and options you will be more apt to react quickly.

1 Reacting to Phillipe's counter of the guillotine, Rodrigo slips his right arm around Phillipe's left arm and locks his hands together. From this position, he begins to apply pressure to Phillipe's spine with the cervical hold.

2 Phillipe counters the attack by bracing both hands on the mat and pushing off. With this motion, he is able to free his head from under Rodrigo's armpit, releasing the pressure.

3 Rodrigo immediately opens his legs, releasing the full closed guard. He then plants his right foot on the mat and pushes off, thus shifting his hips to his right. At the same time, Rodrigo maintains control over Phillipe's left arm by sliding the nook of his right elbow toward Phillipe's elbow. Rodrigo further traps Phillipe's arm by cocking his head to his right.

Elbow should be on top of oppenent's elbow.

4 Rodrigo places his left foot against Phillipe's right hip while taking a small step back with his right foot. Rodrigo pushes off his feet to further escape his hips to the right and move his torso away from Phillipe. This forces Phillipe to extend his body forward and to fully extend his left arm, while being off balance at the same time. Notice that as Rodrigo escapes his torso, he also turns to his left. This is very important, as he needs to create the distance to extend Phillipe's arm.

5 Rodrigo curls his right leg and loops it over Phillipe's left arm, pressing it down on Phillipe's shoulder to keep him trapped. It is very important for Rodrigo to press his legs together; this both traps Phillipe and adds pressure to the lock. Rodrigo uses both his hands to pull down on Phillipe's elbow to accomplish the hyperextension and the arm bar.

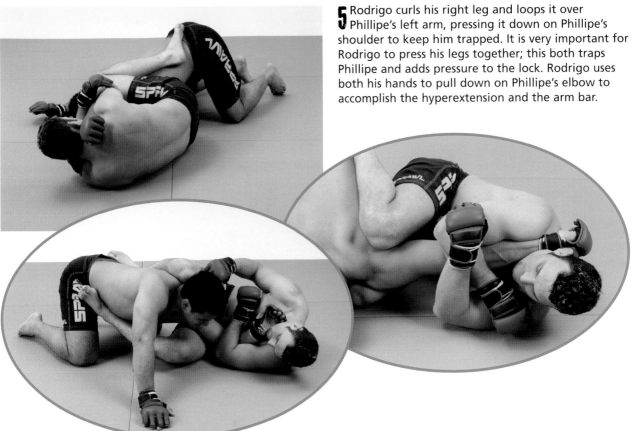

5 Reverse detail Notice Rodrigo's right knee position, on top of Phillipe's left shoulder. Also, you can see how he ensures Phillipe's submission by using two different options: he pulls down with both hands on Phillipe's elbow; and he draws his right arm over with his left hand, helping add pressure. Although both of these options work, the second one is Rodrigo's preference. He believes it not only adds more pressure, but also prevents Phillipe from escaping, which sometimes occurs with the first option. It is important for Rodrigo to curl his torso slightly, in order to add pressure on Phillipe's forearm. To prevent Phillipe from spinning his hand and escaping the pressure (see technique 33), Rodrigo presses his head toward his right shoulder, trapping the hand.

Opponent counters the arm bar 1: rear-mount and choke

At times when faced with this type of arm bar, the opponent is able to spin his wrist and bend his elbow, taking away the pressure on the joint. In that case, Rodrigo follows to the back mount and a rear naked choke.

1 Rodrigo applies the arm bar, as in the previous technique.

2 Phillipe quickly spins his left wrist and bends his elbow down, thereby eliminating the pressure on the joint.

3 Sensing that he lost the lock, Rodrigo imme-diately changes to taking the back. He quickly locks his right hand on Phillipe's right armpit, digging his fingers in as if they were a meat hook. At the same time, Rodrigo releases his left foot from Phillipe's hip, and extends his right leg to loop it over Phillipe's back. In this way, Rodrigo begins to circle his body around Phillipe's torso.

3 Detail Notice how Rodrigo digs his right fingers into Phillipe's right side to help pull himself around to the back. It is also very important for Rodrigo to main-tain his left heel on Phillipe's right hip; otherwise Phillipe will just jump over Rodrigo's leg.

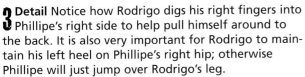

4 Rodrigo props his left elbow on the ground, raising his torso as he works his way toward Phillipe's back.

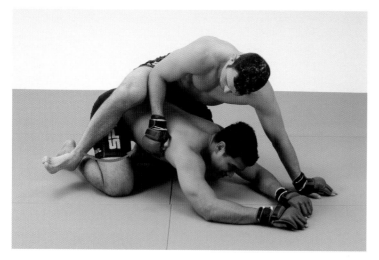

5 Rodrigo continues to slide his body onto Phillipe's back. His left leg is in contact with Phillipe's body until his knee touches the mat. At this point, the left hook is in place. As he reaches Phillipe's back, Rodrigo extends his left arm to help bring his hips square.

6 Rodrigo loops his right leg in, hooking his right foot inside Phillipe's right thigh.

7 Since his left arm was on the ground, Rodrigo wraps it around Phillipe's neck and grabs the top of Phillipe's right shoulder.

8 Rodrigo bends his right arm and slides his right hand behind Phillipe's head. He also locks his left hand on his own right biceps as he sinks the rear naked choke.

8 Detail Notice how Rodrigo slides his right hand over his left one, and locks his left hand onto his right biceps. By bending and sliding the hand in, Rodrigo is able to use a shortcut for this attack. The longer version would be to lock his hand with his right arm extended, and then bend the arm. That method takes longer, and it has another drawback. Because of the gloves in NHB, an opponent can more easily grab the extended arm and block the choke. When you try this move, make sure you place your hand behind your opponent's neck, and not on top of his head, where your opponent may be able to grab the glove and pull your hand off.

9 Rodrigo applies the choke by bringing his elbows together and pulling them toward his chest, squeezing Phillipe's neck.

Opponent counters the arm bar 2: armlock

Another great option to use when the opponent escapes the arm bar is to go for a standard armlock from the guard. Rodrigo already has control over Phillipe's left arm. He can apply the previous technique and go for the back, or, in case Phillipe braces and pushes up to prevent Rodrigo from going to his back, he will create the necessary space and expose the left arm for the armlock.

1 Phillipe has already rotated his left wrist, which allowed him to bend his elbow and escape the arm bar from technique 32. Therefore, Rodrigo starts to move to the back. He hooks his right hand on Phillipe's right armpit. Sensing Rodrigo's attack, Phillipe plants his right hand on the ground and pushes off.

2 Phillipe continues the defense by opening his right leg and pushing up. This creates space between their torsos, which allows Rodrigo to rotate his hips out to his right, while also opening both legs in preparation for the armlock on the left arm. Notice that at no time has Rodrigo released control over Phillipe's arm.

128

3 Rodrigo hooks his left leg on the back of Phillipe's right side, pressing down to keep Phillipe from standing up and pulling away. At the same time, Rodrigo uses his right hand to pull down on Phillipe's right shoulder until he can lock his left leg in place. He also uses his right forearm to brace, keeping Phillipe's head away.

3 **Side view** Notice how Rodrigo's torso is positioned at a 90-degree angle from Phillipe's, and how he uses his right forearm to keep Phillipe's head away.

4 Rodrigo loops his right leg over Phillipe's head to press it down. Rodrigo applies the armlock by extending his leg and driving his hips up against Phillipe's elbow, which hyperextends it.

Guard attack: trapping the arm to triangle

If properly used, the closed guard is a very effective controlling position in NHB. It is also a great place from which to deliver various submission attacks and strikes. While in the past the guard caused confusion to NHB fighters not familiar with jiu-jitsu, over the years various counters to the traditional guard have evolved, including the ground-n-pound, slamming the opponent, and other strike alternatives. In response to that, a new "modern" style of closed guard has developed. Some of the keys to the modern closed guard are controlling the opponent's arms, maintaining his head close to your head and chest to prevent him from getting proper distance to deliver strikes, and angling your body in relation to the opponent so he can't get a direct target to strike. In this technique, Rodrigo uses many of the modern closed-guard principles and attacks Phillipe with a triangle.

1 Rodrigo has Phillipe in his closed guard. Notice that he has wrapped Phillipe's left arm with his right arm, while his left hand prevents Phillipe from punching by blocking Phillipe's right biceps. Also notice how Rodrigo's body is at an angle to Phillipe's, with his hip slightly out toward the right side. This not only puts Phillipe slightly off balance, but also removes Rodrigo's face as a direct target for Phillipe's punches.

2 As Phillipe starts to brace and raise his torso, to center himself so he can strike, Rodrigo slides his left hand from the biceps to control Phillipe's wrist.

3 Detail Notice how Rodrigo grabs his left wrist with his right hand, allowing for ultimate control over Phillipe's arms. Also notice Rodrigo's torso position in relation to Phillipe's. His head is out to his own right, and he has turned his chest in to facilitate reaching the grip. By sliding his hip toward his own right, Rodrigo makes it easier to loop his leg over Phillipe's right arm. Notice how Rodrigo pushes Phillipe's right wrist in with his left hand.

3 Rodrigo pushes Phillipe's right wrist in slightly and across his stomach, so he can grab his own left wrist with his right hand. Notice that Rodrigo's torso has moved in and out to help this sequence. As Phillipe started to brace, and tried to center, Rodrigo's torso was slightly more in, and also in front of Phillipe; as soon as Rodrigo controlled the wrist with his left hand, Rodrigo twisted his torso back to his right to facilitate his reaching his left wrist. Notice that without this body movement, it might have been hard for Rodrigo to simply push a stronger opponent's arm in. This way, the technique will work against an opponent of any size.

4 Having completely locked Phillipe's arms, Rodrigo can open his legs wide without fear of losing control, and without Phillipe passing the guard. Rodrigo then opens his legs and loops the left leg over Phillipe's right arm and shoulder. Notice that Rodrigo has to let go of Phillipe's right wrist as soon as he passes the left leg over; otherwise, he cannot close the leg, or it would be over his own left arm as well.

5 Rodrigo locks his left leg tight around Phillipe's neck, pressing the heel toward his own torso to keep Phillipe from pulling away. At the same time, Rodrigo places his right foot on Phillipe's left hip, and pushes off in order to raise his hips. This makes it easier to lock the triangle. Notice how Rodrigo's left hand is again blocking Phillipe's right arm. When you try this move, remember that any time you are applying the triangle, the opponent can and will strike with punches with the arm that is not trapped. Always account for this, and block it.

6 With his right hand, Rodrigo grabs his left ankle and pulls it down, cinching the control. Notice that Rodrigo is still careful, and blocks Phillipe's right arm.

7 Rodrigo locks the figure-four around Phillipe's left arm and head, by locking his right leg over his left ankle. Rodrigo pulls down with both hands on Phillipe's head, as he closes his knees together to apply the choking pressure.

Guard attack: triangle

The triangle is always a great attack from the closed guard. It is even better at times in NHB matches when the opponent is trying to free his arm for a punch. In this case, Rodrigo has trapped Phillipe's left arm and uses Phillipe's motion to free his arm to initiate the triangle attack.

1 Rodrigo has Phillipe in his closed guard, with the left arm trapped by Rodrigo's right arm. Rodrigo's hips are escaped to his left side, and he holds the back of Phillipe's head with his left hand. The closer Rodrigo keeps Phillipe's torso to him, the more attack options he has. This also removes Phillipe's ability to punch.

2 Phillipe wants to throw a punch, so he braces his left hand on the ground and pushes off it, in order to slide the arm out.

3 Sensing that he is losing control of the arm, and that a punch might be coming, Rodrigo hooks his right hand on Phillipe's arm. Notice that Rodrigo uses a bent arm, with the forearm pressing against Phillipe's biceps, to block Phillipe from delivering a short punch. He also uses his right thigh to trap Phillipe's arm from going back, which prevents him from looping a big punch.

4 Still in control of Phillipe's left arm, because his right hand is hooked around Phillipe's elbow, Rodrigo coils his right leg, puts his foot on Phillipe's left hip, and slides his knee in front of Phillipe's arm. At this point, Phillipe can neither punch nor free his arm. Also notice how Rodrigo's left hand remains in control of the back of Phillipe's neck, and that his left leg is hooked on the back, to keep Phillipe from standing up and stepping away. In this way, Rodrigo has the fight on the ground, where he wants to be; he does not want to give Phillipe a chance to get back up.

5 Rodrigo slides his right hand from Phillipe's elbow down to his wrist, and then he grabs it. At the same time, he shifts his hips away and to the center. He continues to slide his right leg in, now with the shin pressing against Phillipe's biceps.

6 Rodrigo opens Phillipe's left arm out by pushing Phillipe's wrist to the right with his right hand. This creates space for his right foot to go in and around Phillipe's left arm. Notice that Rodrigo has cocked his right leg in order to be able to bring his foot all the way inside the arm. At this point, Rodrigo can either place the foot against Phillipe's biceps, while holding the wrist, and punch with the left hand, or he can just go for the triangle choke as he slips the foot in.

7 Rodrigo loops his right leg around Phillipe's neck and uses his left hand to grab his right ankle, thereby locking the position. Note that Rodrigo still has control of Phillipe's left wrist, in order to keep him from punching.

8c Rodrigo puts his left foot on Phillipe's right hip and uses it to spin his body to his right, creating a better angle for his leg to lock down on Phillipe. This is a subtle yet important detail, especially for people with shorter legs. By keeping hips facing an opponent, it makes it much harder to cinch the triangle. Notice that Rodrigo's right hand still controls Phillipe's left wrist, and his left hand is pulling his right ankle down, to keep the lock tight.

8c Reverse angle Notice how Rodrigo locks his left hand onto his right ankle. He has released his left leg, which had been hooked on Phillipe's back, and placed the foot on Phillipe's hip to help him turn his torso to his right to create a better angle for the triangle and to keep Phillipe's hips away from his hips. Should he allow Phillipe to bring his hips in close, Phillipe will be able to posture and defend. By keeping him away and falling forward, Rodrigo foils Phillipe's counter option.

9 Rodrigo loops his left leg over his right foot and presses his knees together for the figure-four lock. By pulling the back of Phillipe's head down with his hands, he also sinks the triangle choke.

Guard attack: armless triangle

A common and effective way to pass the guard is for the opponent to use both arms to underhook the defender's legs. Once he achieves that kind of control, Phillipe would simply pull the hips up tight, then stack Rodrigo, choose one side, and pass to that side under and around the leg. Should Rodrigo fail to counter, Phillipe would pass his guard and reach side-control. In that case, Rodrigo likes to use this choke to finish his opponent.

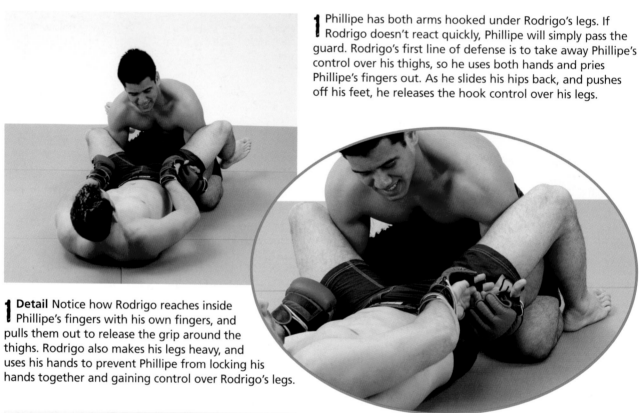

1 Phillipe has both arms hooked under Rodrigo's legs. If Rodrigo doesn't react quickly, Phillipe will simply pass the guard. Rodrigo's first line of defense is to take away Phillipe's control over his thighs, so he uses both hands and pries Phillipe's fingers out. As he slides his hips back, and pushes off his feet, he releases the hook control over his legs.

1 Detail Notice how Rodrigo reaches inside Phillipe's fingers with his own fingers, and pulls them out to release the grip around the thighs. Rodrigo also makes his legs heavy, and uses his hands to prevent Phillipe from locking his hands together and gaining control over Rodrigo's legs.

2 Pushing off his right foot, Rodrigo slides his hips to his right, and brings his left leg over Phillipe's right shoulder. He locks it around the back of Phillipe's neck at the same time Rodrigo slides his left forearm over his left thigh, and under Phillipe's chin. Notice that it is very important for Rodrigo to have created the space by pushing back off his feet in step one, otherwise Phillipe could simply throw his right leg over and pass the guard. The distance created, however, prevents Phillipe from doing that, as he is too far away to have the leverage and proper position to throw the leg and pass. This is a moment of vulnerability in this attack. When you try this move, make sure you have the proper hip distance, and that you act quickly.

3 Rodrigo turns his torso to his left a little more. From here, he locks Phillipe's head in by locking his left forearm under Phillipe's chin. He also pulls down on his left ankle with his right hand, applying pressure on the back of Phillipe's neck and forcing it down.

4 Rodrigo pulls the left ankle down with his right hand, until he can reach it with his left hand. Rodrigo then pulls down on the left ankle with his left hand, choking Phillipe. Notice how Rodrigo's left hand comes in to grab the ankle. The hand comes on the inside, and reaches around the outside of the ankle with its palm facing Rodrigo's head. Rodrigo needs to see the tip of his fingers; otherwise, the grip is incorrect. This forces the upper blade of the forearm against Phillipe's throat.

5 Rodrigo locks his right leg over his left foot to finish the triangle. Notice that since Phillipe has no arms inside the triangle, Rodrigo's left arm replaces Phillipe's left arm. Rodrigo's forearm applies pressure to the left side of Phillipe's throat, while the biceps and thigh press against the left side for the choking pressure. Rodrigo closes his knees together and brings them toward his chest to add the triangle choking pressure.

Guard replacement with heel strike

A fight is an unpredictable chain of events guided by the willpower of two men and their trained reactions. You may find yourself at times in a less than auspicious position, such as being on the ground with the opponent standing in front of you, ready to pass or kick. Rodrigo has already shown one way to maintain safe distance and stand up in base. This time, however, the attacker is able to avoid the defense and get to Rodrigo's side, pushing his legs out of the way. One of the best ways to recover from such a position is shown here.

1 Phillipe stands in front of Rodrigo, who is on his back in a defensive position with his legs cocked. His hands are holding Phillipe's shins, and he is ready to release a heel strike to Phillipe's knees.

2 Phillipe somehow avoids the strike, and manages to get past Rodrigo's legs. He is passing the guard by pushing Rodrigo's knees away to the right, as he moves to his left. If Rodrigo does not react, Phillipe will either reach side-control, knee-on-stomach, or even deliver a kick to the face, as shown in technique 53. Since Phillipe has pushed Rodrigo's legs so far over, Rodrigo cannot escape his hips and replace the guard. Therefore, he has to roll over.

3 Rodrigo immediately circles his legs around his head, as he rolls over his right shoulder. Notice that Rodrigo extends his legs out, and draws a semi-circle with his feet, until they are almost straight over his head. He then returns his legs back in front. Notice that Rodrigo touches the tip of his left foot on the mat to help propel his legs back.

4 Pushing off his left foot, Rodrigo brings his legs back over, and around to the front center. Notice that Rodrigo makes a big circle with his right leg, while maintaining his left one between himself and Phillipe, which prevents Phillipe from coming close.

5 Having completed the move, Rodrigo ends up back in the open guard, with his left foot pushing against Phillipe's right hip. His right leg is open, and both hands are holding onto Phillipe's left arm. Rodrigo now grabs Phillipe's right arm—the arm on the same side of Phillipe's body that Rodrigo's foot presses.

6 Rodrigo continues his body rotation to his right, and then switches his left foot for the right one, which has been pressing against Phillipe's left hip. He pushes the hip back, as he pulls forward on the arm. Rodrigo coils his left leg back.

7 Rodrigo then delivers a heel strike to Phillipe's chin. This is a very powerful strike, as Phillipe cannot step back to diminish it, and therefore has to absorb its full impact with his jaw.

GROUND FIGHTING

Open Guard

While in the closed guard one generally looks for closeness, the opposite is true in the open guard. Of course, you do not want your opponent so far away that you cannot have any contact or control over him, in which case you would execute a "stand-up in base" technique.

In an NHB open guard, first you worry about protecting yourself by not giving your opponent the chance to strike you, especially in the face. Once you have assured your safety, there are many options available, as Rodrigo will demonstrate.

Gaining the open guard

Many times when an opponent is in your guard, he may want to remain there, either to allow the round to end or to throw punches. Either way, you may want to achieve a more active position, such as the open guard. Here, Rodrigo shows how to open the guard safely and attain a more aggressive open guard stance while still preventing your opponent from striking you.

1 Phillipe is in Rodrigo's guard, but he has managed to free his head and gain posture. From here, he can deliver punches, or just wait until the round ends. Rodrigo wants to press the action, but still protect himself, so he keeps both hands on Phillipe's shoulders, ready to block any punches.

2 Rodrigo unlocks his feet, releasing the closed guard. He plants his right foot out and pushes off, pivoting his hips to the right and sliding his right hand down toward Phillipe's left triceps.

3 Phillipe may loop in a left punch, so Rodrigo keeps his right knee and right elbow connected to block any such punches. Notice how Rodrigo has his right arm bent at the elbow, using his forearm to block Phillipe's punch. Also notice that Rodrigo's right hand is cupped as if it were a hook.

4 Having blocked Phillipe's punch, Rodrigo hooks his right hand on Phillipe's arm and circles his right arm around to the right. This pulls Phillipe's left arm to the outside of his right knee. Rodrigo then puts his left foot on Phillipe's right hip, to control the distance. Notice that Rodrigo controls Phillipe's left elbow, to prevent him from bringing his arm out to throw another punch.

5 Pushing off his left foot, Rodrigo centers his hips, and then creates more distance between himself and Phillipe by pushing away. At this point, Rodrigo pushes against Phillipe's hips with both feet; his right hand controls Phillipe's left arm by bracing the shin against the biceps. Now Phillipe's only attacking option is to throw a right punch. Again Rodrigo has a great defensive posture, with his left elbow touching the top of his left knee, and his left arm bent, with the forearm blocking the punch and the hand cupped like a hook.

6 Before Phillipe's punch gets near Rodrigo's face, Rodrigo has pushed off his legs and has turned to the right, which removes much of Phillipe's punching power. Phillipe's punch meets Rodrigo's block.

7 Rodrigo cups his left hand over Phillipe's right arm, and then pulls it around and down to the outside of his left leg. Now Rodrigo has a defensive open guard with his shins pressing against Phillipe's biceps and his hands controlling the back of the arms at the triceps, making it very difficult for Phillipe to launch any punches. Rodrigo is ready to make things happen.

Open-guard attack: heel hook

The heel hook is a devastatingly effective submission. With its attacks on the knee and the ankle joints at the same time, the heel hook usually does severe damage to the knee before the defender even realizes the danger. Because of the extensive damage it can cause, the heel hook is considered illegal in some events. It is always an option from the open guard. If it is allowed, it is a formidable fight ender, so look for it.

1 Rodrigo has Phillipe in his open guard. He is using an outside hook guard, where his left hand grabs the back of Phillipe's right heel. Rodrigo's left leg hooks around the outside of Phillipe's right leg, until his foot hooks right inside the thigh. With his right foot pushing against Phillipe's ribs, Rodrigo maintains distance and control, so Phillipe cannot kick him with his right leg. Rodrigo's right hand grabs Phillipe's right wrist, preventing him from punching.

2 Phillipe postures and counters Rodrigo's position by leaning forward and driving his right knee forward. If Rodrigo does not react, Phillipe may be able to deflect Rodrigo's right leg and break the defensive barrier.

3 Sensing he is losing the controlling edge, Rodrigo releases the left foot hook and loops his leg over and around Phillipe's right leg.

4 Rodrigo continues to circle his right leg around Phillipe's leg, until he can bring his left knee in under Phillipe's leg, right next to Phillipe's calf. Notice that at this point, Rodrigo's left leg is now completely under Phillipe's right leg. So, in effect, Rodrigo has circled his leg all the way around Phillipe's right leg.

5 Rodrigo finishes circling his leg around Phillipe's right leg when he locks the left foot inside Phillipe's right hip. At this point, having achieved another controlling position where Phillipe cannot advance or strike him, Rodrigo releases his right foot from Phillipe's ribs, and places it on Phillipe's left knee. He also applies pressure with his left leg, driving his heel to the ground and pushing in his knee.

5 **Reverse angle** Notice Rodrigo's left leg position, looped around Phillipe's right leg. Also, notice how he uses his right foot to push just behind Phillipe's left knee, causing the leg to open.

146

6 Rodrigo extends his right leg, pushing Phillipe's left knee and leg out. At the same time, he presses his left leg forward and down, causing Phillipe to fall forward and catch himself with his left hand. Rodrigo still maintains control over Phillipe's right hand, with his own hand. Notice that at this point, Phillipe's right leg is turning in, with the heel pointing up, as a consequence of Rodrigo's actions. Rodrigo then wraps his left arm under Phillipe's right ankle, locking it in the nook of his elbow and locking the top of Phillipe's right foot with his armpit. Rodrigo makes sure his left elbow is tight against his body, in order to lock the foot and ankle in place.

7 Rodrigo releases Phillipe's right hand, and locks it under his left wrist. He then applies the heel hook by pulling his arm in toward his right, making sure not to open the elbow out and thereby release the lock on Phillipe's heel. Notice that Rodrigo continues to push Phillipe's left knee away with his right leg.

7 Detail Notice Rodrigo's grip around Phillipe's ankle, and how his left arm hooks under and around the ankle; the elbow nook locks tight. The right hand grabs under the left hand, and pulls the hand up toward the right, causing the forearm to torque Phillipe's ankle around.

Open-guard attack: heel-hook defense

Since the heel hook is so common and dangerous from the open guard, you need to have an equally effective counter ready in case your opponent attempts to use one during a fight. The key to this defense, like all other moves, is timing, but in this case the submission is so damaging that you especially need to react quickly and forcefully.

1 Phillipe has Rodrigo in his open guard, with his leg wrapped around the outside. He goes for a heel hook.

2 After seeing Phillipe's left leg begin to circle around his right leg, Rodrigo knows the heel hook is coming. Therefore, he immediately pushes off the ball of his right foot, and turns his body around to his left (the direction of the pressure on his knee), so that his right knee points away from Phillipe. With this movement, the right foot has completely turned, with the top facing away from Phillipe's head. This prevents Phillipe from effectively trapping Rodrigo's toes under his armpit, which keeps Rodrigo's foot free, and not locked by Phillipe's left elbow and armpit.

3 Rodrigo drops to the mat, posts both arms out, and cocks his left leg. He puts his foot right against Phillipe's left buttock.

4 Rodrigo extends his left leg, pushing Phillipe away as he pulls his right leg out. This releases his foot, and allows him to escape the heel hook.

5 Rodrigo steps forward with his right leg, and gets ready to stand up to reengage Phillipe.

Open-guard attack: triangle

Maintaining control of your opponent and protecting yourself from receiving strikes is the number one concern in an NHB match. All the techniques in the world will not help you if you get caught square with a knockout punch or kick. Here, Rodrigo achieved the open guard as in the previous technique, but Phillipe managed to stand up, so Rodrigo has to adjust his position. Rodrigo starts with a defensive open guard. When the opponent stands up, once Rodrigo's control and safety is secure, he opens up for the triangle attack. In this technique Rodrigo demonstrates several things: the proper way to control the opponent, a great way to block punches from the open guard, and a great attack.

1 Although Rodrigo had achieved open guard and generally good control over Phillipe, as in the previous technique, Phillipe has nevertheless managed to stand up. Notice that Rodrigo's hands are still controlling Phillipe's elbows, and his legs press out, to prevent Phillipe from freeing his arm and throwing a punch.

2 Rodrigo quickly releases the grip on Phillipe's right arm, changing both hands to Phillipe's left wrist. He also pushes off his right foot, sending Phillipe back off balance, and creating distance so that Phillipe cannot punch him. Notice that Rodrigo's left leg is cocked and ready. At this point, Rodrigo can throw a left heel kick to Phillipe's face with devastating results.

3 Phillipe regains his balance and moves in. Rodrigo continues controlling Phillipe's left hand, with both hands pulling the wrist down, and he spins his body. As he turns his head to the right, he extends his left leg and pushes the bottom of his foot against Phillipe's biceps, to block that arm. Rodrigo maintains pressure on his right leg, with that foot pushing against Phillipe's left hip, to control the distance.

Drive the heel down to keep the opponent from posturing up.

4 In one movement, Rodrigo pushes off his right foot and raises his hips. He shoots his left foot up, off Phillipe's right biceps. The release of the pressure on Phillipe's right arm, along with Rodrigo's continued pulling of the left wrist, forces Phillipe's torso to bend forward. As Rodrigo pulls Phillipe's wrist across his body, he locks his left leg around the back of Phillipe's neck. Notice that Rodrigo uses his left hand to block any right punches thrown by Phillipe.

5 Rodrigo executes the figure-four by locking his right leg at the knee over his left foot, completing the triangle choke. Notice that Rodrigo's left arm is out to block any punches that Phillipe may attempt with his right arm.

6 Rodrigo applies a choking pressure with his hands by pulling down on Phillipe's head; he also brings his knees together to add pressure.

Open-guard attack: omoplata

Another great option for an open-guard attack when controlling the arms to prevent punches is the omoplata (shoulder lock). The omoplata, the triangle, and the armlock are related; one attack actually sets up the other, or the same setup can work for different attacks depending on the opponent's reaction. In this case, Rodrigo starts with the same controlling open guard as before and goes for the omoplata, but he could have used the same setup to go for the triangle, making some slight adjustments to the move in technique 45.

1 Rodrigo controls Phillipe's arms in the open guard.

2 Pushing off his right foot, Rodrigo shifts his hips away and to his left, while pulling Phillipe's right elbow with his left hand. He also slides his left leg out and under, which extends Phillipe's right arm.

3 Rodrigo circles his left leg around Phillipe's right arm, while still controlling Phillipe's elbow with his left hand. At this point, Rodrigo's torso is also circling towards his left to help set up the omoplata attack.

4 Rodrigo plants and pushes off his right foot, which forces his torso to circle to his left. At the same time, he completely circles his left leg around Phillipe's right arm. Notice that Rodrigo has slid his left hand from Phillipe's elbow and down to his wrist. This helps him maintain control over Phillipe's right arm; otherwise Phillipe could just pull his arm out.

5 Having achieved the proper position for the omoplata, and being certain that Phillipe's arm is secured, Rodrigo releases Phillipe's wrist and places his free left hand against Phillipe's right hip. He also scoots his own hip away from Phillipe, which prevents Phillipe from getting close to Rodrigo. If Phillipe gets close, he can defend the lock, by jumping over Rodrigo's head, or counter, by sitting up and achieving a defensive posture that would allow him to roll Rodrigo over his own head. Rodrigo prevents this by extending his left leg and pushing Phillipe's shoulder and torso down.

5 Reverse angle Notice how Rodrigo places his stiff right arm against Phillipe's left hip, allowing him to block Phillipe from circling and jumping over Rodrigo's head to counter the attack.

6 Rodrigo kicks his left heel to the ground, forcing Phillipe to go head down against the mat. Notice that Rodrigo's left arm now controls Phillipe's left hip. This prevents Phillipe from rolling forward over his right shoulder to counter the attack, releasing the pressure on his shoulder. Notice that as Rodrigo progresses in the attack, Phillipe's escape options change and become more and more limited.

7 Rodrigo hooks his left arm under Phillipe's left armpit, grabs Phillipe's shoulder, and sits forward. This allows his torso to force Phillipe's right forearm forward, torquing his shoulder. It is important that Phillipe's right shoulder touches the ground, preventing him from posturing, standing up, and throwing Rodrigo back.

8 Some people have more flexibility than others; if Phillipe has extremely limber shoulders, Rodrigo can also punch Phillipe in the face from this controlling position.

Open-guard attack: omoplata to footlock

One of the counters to the omoplata is for the opponent to circle over the attacker's head, reaching the other side of the body and foiling the attack. Here, Rodrigo prevents that by using a stiff arm against the hip to maintain distance, but at times he may be late or the opponent may somehow manage to release the block and proceed with the counter. In that case, Rodrigo has another attack ready: the footlock!

1 Rodrigo places his stiff right arm against Phillipe's left hip. This allows him to block Phillipe from circling and jumping over Rodrigo's head to counter the attack.

2 Phillipe somehow is able to fend off the block, and he begins to step around Rodrigo's head. If he manages to get completely around to Rodrigo's left side, he will have defended the lock and end up in an advantageous position. Therefore, Rodrigo uses his left hand against Phillipe's left knee to slow his progress.

The right hand secures the oppenent's foot.

3 Rodrigo turns his hips out to the left as he releases his right hand from Phillipe's hip, and then places it inside and around Phillipe's right ankle. At the same time, Rodrigo turns his torso to his right, and reaches with his left hand around Phillipe's calf. He continues until he can lock his left hand onto his own right wrist.

4 Rodrigo slides his right hand from Phillipe's ankle down to his toes in order to apply the toe hold. He pulls Phillipe's toes around with his right hand.

4 Detail Notice how Rodrigo's right hand holds Phillipe's left foot on the outside by his toes. To apply the toe-hold pressure, Rodrigo will pull the toes toward his own right elbow, forcing the foot to pivot around the ankle.

5 If Rodrigo fails to stop Phillipe, Phillipe will continue on to Rodrigo's left side, and defend the omoplata attack.

Open-guard attack: omoplata to triangle

It is very important to maintain distance from your opponent as you go for the omoplata, otherwise your opponent has many options to counter it. Some fighters actually plant their foot (as in technique 46, step 5) and scoot out several times, forcing the opponent's shoulder down to the mat and moving away to prevent these counters. The other option for Phillipe to counter the omoplata is to sit up, forcing Rodrigo to roll over his own right shoulder. Once again, Rodrigo is ready for the counter and changes back to the omoplata's cousin, the triangle.

1 Rodrigo places his stiff right arm against Phillipe's left hip. This blocks Phillipe from circling and jumping over Rodrigo's head to counter the attack.

2 Phillipe, however, was able to lock his hands together, posture up, and raise his torso. In this way, Phillipe tries to force Rodrigo to roll over his right shoulder.

3 Rodrigo immediately releases the omoplata lock and spreads his legs to keep Phillipe from rolling him over. Rodrigo uses his right leg as a pivot point to help bring himself to center, so he is facing Phillipe again. He pushes off the right leg, pressing against Phillipe's side, and swings his torso to the left.

4 Using the momentum of the push off his right leg, Rodrigo raises his hips and brings his left leg back in, locking it over Phillipe's right shoulder. Rodrigo then places his right foot on Phillipe's left hip, lifting his hips high, until they are pressing against Phillipe's neck. This not only helps the tightness of the attack, but it also helps Rodrigo's left leg to lock better around Phillipe's neck. Notice that Phillipe's arm is on Rodrigo's right side, and he needs to bring it to the left for the triangle. He reaches with the left hand to grab Phillipe's elbow.

5 With his left hand, Rodrigo pulls Phillipe's left arm across his body and grabs his own left ankle with his right hand. By doing this, Rodrigo controls the hold and is able to make the necessary adjustments, so that he can lock his right leg over his left ankle. Should Rodrigo not hold the ankle, he would actually have to rely only on the leg pressure against the back of Phillipe's neck to keep him close. Rodrigo keeps his right foot pushing against Phillipe's left hip to keep him away and slightly off balance.

6 Rodrigo locks the figure-four around Phillipe's head and left arm, by locking his right leg over his left ankle. He applies the choking pressure by bringing his knees together, and using both hands to pull Phillipe's head down to his body.

Open-guard attack: heel kick

The heel kick to the face is an extremely powerful strike when executed from the guard. Since the opponent's face is at a perfect distance and your leg power thrusting forward is very strong, the effects can be devastating. Rodrigo demonstrates one way to deliver the kick, starting from the same open guard as the previous attacks. At the highest levels of competition, the winning difference will be the ability of a fighter to have a strong set of options from a certain position.

1 Rodrigo has Phillipe in his open guard.

2 Rodrigo creates distance from Phillipe by pushing off his legs. Notice that if Phillipe is a bigger person, Rodrigo moves away; if the two men are the same weight, Rodrigo will be capable of pushing Phillipe away with his legs. Rodrigo changes both hands to grip Phillipe's right wrist. At the same time, he pushes off his left foot (still on Phillipe's right hip), and turns his body to his left while cocking his right leg. Notice that by pushing off the leg and turning the body, Rodrigo creates the proper distance for the strike. If he had stayed square with Phillipe, he wouldn't have had enough distance for his leg to fully extend and achieve maximum striking power.

3 While still holding Phillipe's right arm, Rodrigo thrusts his right heel forward, striking Phillipe's jaw. By holding onto Phillipe's hand, Rodrigo intensifies the strike; Phillipe cannot move back fully, and therefore absorbs the impact of the strike. Rodrigo makes sure to strike with the heel of his foot, the harder part.

Open-guard attack: heel strike–scissor sweep combination

Continuing with our multiple options from the guard, Rodrigo demonstrates the heel strike–scissor sweep combination. The heel strike will not only cause damage to Phillipe's face but will also distract him, allowing Rodrigo to execute the scissor sweep.

1 Starting from the open guard, Phillipe is able to free his arms from Rodrigo's total control. In this way, he starts to pass the guard, by pushing down on Rodrigo's left knee.

2 Rodrigo immediately reacts by sliding his hands from Phillipe's elbows, down to his wrists. He then pulls Phillipe's right hand from his left knee, and places his right knee in front of Phillipe's chest, blocking his forward path.

3 Rodrigo places his right foot on Phillipe's left hip, releases the left foot from Phillipe's right hip, and swings his left leg out. Notice that Rodrigo is on his left side, and that his foot swings to the left, with the heel pointing in.

4 Rodrigo quickly brings his heel in, striking Phillipe's right jaw. Notice that Rodrigo still controls both of Phillipe's arms, with his hands on Phillipe's wrists, as he pulls the arms forward. This inhibits Phillipe's balance, as well as preventing his ability to easily stand up. Rodrigo's heel strike to the face will force Phillipe to lower his head, making it easier for Rodrigo to sweep.

5 Following the quick strike, Rodrigo swings his left leg out and circles it back in again. This time, he slides it along the mat and strikes Phillipe's right leg, taking away Phillipe's base. At the same time, Rodrigo pulls forward on Phillipe's arm, and takes it across his body. He also kicks in his right leg, making a scissor motion with his legs.

6 Rodrigo follows Phillipe's momentum, and ends up in the mounted position. Notice that Rodrigo still controls Phillipe's wrists. With his left hand, Rodrigo then pushes down on Phillipe's right arm, clearing a path for the punch.

7 Rodrigo releases his right hand grip, cocks that arm, and punches over Phillipe's arms, striking his face.

GROUND FIGHTING

Passing the Guard

Passing the guard in a street fight or an NHB match requires some very specific skills. In sports jiu-jitsu and submission grappling it is important to attain proper posture and have patience before you attempt to pass someone's guard. The same is true in NHB. It is especially important to avoid submissions and proceed only when you are certain that all the elements such as posture and control are in place before you begin your guard passes. You need to have all the same tools that are required of a sports jiu-jitsu fighter, such as patience, avoiding submissions, and so on, and in addition you need to have even better posture since you cannot rely on the gi to brace your arms.

Because of the dangers of strikes, whether from punches from the bottom or heel kicks to the face, passing the guard in NHB is a very risky proposition and should be given the proper respect. The first rule of NHB guard passing is to protect yourself at all times. If you have to risk getting hit to achieve a positional gain, consider all the possibilities first and then weigh the risk and reward. If you risk a knock-out to advance, is it worth it?

To pass someone's guard, you must first achieve posture and avoid submissions. After you are sure of your position, have patience and be ready to return to a safer position should something be out of place or appear risky. Then dispose of all the blocks and obstacles that are in your way and control your opponent's ability to move his hips and gain distance.

Don't forget that you are in an NHB fight and use strikes to your advantage to distract your opponent or to finish a fight. Remember, because he is worried about defending the pass, there will be openings to strike. Look for them and take advantage of them as you feel comfortable. This will add another element for your opponent to have to consider and will make your guard-passing task slightly easier.

NHB guard-pass posture

Because of your opponent's ability to throw punches in NHB, your posture in the guard has to be slightly modified from the jiu-jitsu standard.

1 Rodrigo is inside Phillipe's guard. Notice that his hands are cupping Phillipe's biceps, preventing Phillipe from punching. From this position, Rodrigo can do two things: his hand can stop Phillipe's arm from circling up and freeing itself; and his elbow can stop Phillipe from trying to circle his arms around the bottom to free them. Rodrigo keeps his legs close, with the thighs controlling Phillipe's hips to keep him from moving them to the sides and creating angles of attack.

1 **Top view** Notice how Rodrigo cups Phillipe's biceps.

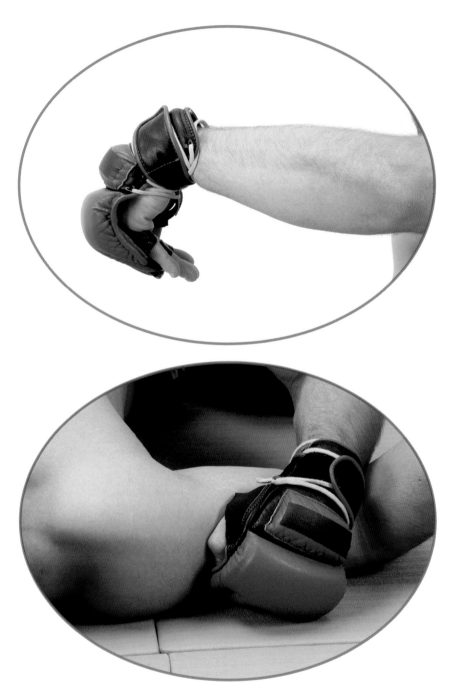

1 Detail Check out Rodrigo's hand position, which allows him to cup Phillipe's arm so that Phillipe cannot circle it in an upward direction.

Opponent on his back 1: passing the guard to knee-on-stomach

Being able to cross the opponent's defensive barrier is an objective in any fight. Here, Rodrigo is standing and Phillipe is on the ground with a very good defensive position, but he is worried about Rodrigo's strikes. Rodrigo takes advantage of this, closing the distance and using Phillipe's reaction to pass the guard to a knee-on-stomach, where he can deliver strikes.

1 Rodrigo stands in front of Phillipe, who is on his back with good defensive posture. Phillipe can deliver strikes with his legs to keep Rodrigo at a safe distance.

2 Rodrigo takes a big step forward with his right leg, cutting the distance to Phillipe. Timing of the step is critical, as Rodrigo needs to maintain his distance from Phillipe. Therefore, he has to be either too far from, or too close to, the power zone of Phillipe's kick (the distance of his leg extended). In this case, he is too close; because of the lack of distance, Phillipe cannot fully extend his leg and deliver an effective kick to the knee. At this point, Phillipe's only striking option is to kick upwards, aiming at Rodrigo's face. Notice the position of Rodrigo's left hand, which is in front of his face and shielding it from a possible strike from Phillipe. It is important for Rodrigo to keep his weight forward, on his right leg, to keep pressure on Phillipe; otherwise Phillipe could just drive him away with a right leg push against the knee.

3 Since Phillipe cannot kick Rodrigo's leg, he coils his right leg and kicks up towards Rodrigo's face. Rodrigo uses his right hand to deflect Phillipe's foot to the right; at the same time, he steps forward with his right leg, planting his right foot next to Phillipe's right hip. In this way, Phillipe cannot replace his foot on Rodrigo's leg, and Rodrigo has effectively passed the guard. Notice Rodrigo's left hand continues to shield his face from an upward kick by Phillipe.

4 Rodrigo continues to push Phillipe's leg down to his right, effectively spinning Phillipe counterclockwise. Rodrigo drives his right knee forward against Phillipe's right thigh, further forcing the thigh down and creating the opening to get his right knee-on-stomach.

Opponent on his back 2: variation

In the previous technique, Rodrigo took advantage of Phillipe's reaction and passed the guard. As an alternative, and to further create confusion, Rodrigo can use the same principle and strike his opponent. We pick up the position after Rodrigo closes the distance by stepping forward, taking away Phillipe's ability to strike with a low kick.

1 After cutting the distance, Rodrigo positions his right foot next to Phillipe's right hip. Phillipe kicks up, aiming at Rodrigo's face, to protect himself from Rodrigo striking or passing the guard.

2 Rodrigo grips Phillipe's right heel with both hands and lifts it up.

3 Pivoting his right foot and using his hands to propel himself forward, Rodrigo swings his left leg around the outside in order to deliver a spinning kick with his left foot to the right side of Phillipe's face. Many times the opponent is ready and blocks the outside kick, knowing that Rodrigo has the next move ready.

4 As soon as he strikes the outside kick and Phillipe blocks, Rodrigo uses the momentum of the strike and pivots in, circling clockwise and bringing his left leg between his right leg and Phillipe's right leg. Bending his left leg at the knee helps Rodrigo place his left foot inside Phillipe's right leg.

5 Rodrigo extends his left leg and delivers a powerful heel kick to Phillipe's face. Note in this sequence that Rodrigo may do an outside strike the first time, and then come back with another outside strike. As Phillipe blocks, Rodrigo can go for the inside rear kick, or he may fake a third outside strike and immediately come in with the heel strike.

NHB guard pass to kick

Since NHB allows strikes, a smart passer like Rodrigo will take advantage of the rules and introduce mayhem and confusion with a barrage of punches. Rodrigo uses them to his advantage whenever possible, including passing the guard. Here Rodrigo punches Phillipe's face to pass the guard. By using strikes to the face, Rodrigo forces Phillipe to defend, making it easier for him to pass.

1 Rodrigo is inside Phillipe's closed guard. He cups his hands around Phillipe's biceps to prevent him from punching. His knees are close against Phillipe's hips, preventing Phillipe from moving them from side to side. Rodrigo waits here for the moment when Phillipe stops moving and Rodrigo can feel secure to start the pass.

2 In one quick movement, Rodrigo raises his torso and lifts his hips off the ground, placing his right arm on Phillipe's throat and his left arm on Phillipe's hips to prevent Phillipe from raising them for a possible attack. Notice how Rodrigo keeps his back straight and his head up. This creates distance from Phillipe's punches. Also very important: Rodrigo's weight is on his legs and not on his arms. Rodrigo knows that if he uses his arms as a brace, Phillipe can pull them out from under him, causing him to fall. Therefore, he uses his legs as power and bracing points. He places his hand on Phillipe's neck in order to prevent Phillipe from sitting up; he is not placing weight on that hand.

2 Detail Notice Rodrigo's left hand placement: right on the inside of Phillipe's right hip. This prevents Phillipe from rising and adds another brace point for the next step.

3 Rodrigo steps out with his right foot. Notice that Rodrigo steps out with the right leg first because he has his right hand forward against Phillipe's neck. Again, notice Rodrigo's posture, with his back straight. Although he is leaning slightly forward to keep the pressure on Phillipe, his weight is equally distributed between his arms, his right foot, and his left knee. At this point, his hips are slightly higher than in the previous step.

3 Correct Notice how Rodrigo prepares his left foot so that he can stand up. As he steps forward with the right leg, he first circles his left leg out, and then plants his toes on the mat so he is ready to spring up.

3 Incorrect Rodrigo has his left foot flat on the mat, preventing him from being able to spring off his foot.

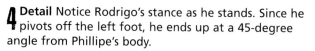

4 Pushing off his legs, Rodrigo stands up and pivots off his left foot. At this point, Rodrigo is safe from the danger of Phillipe's punches, but he is in danger of being hit with kicks, especially a heel strike. Rodrigo therefore keeps his knee in, forcing his thighs against Phillipe's thighs, in order to control Phillipe's legs and prevent kicks. Notice that Rodrigo stands up with his body slightly sideways; he avoids having his feet square with Phillipe's body, because in that stance, he would be off-balance.

4 **Detail** Notice Rodrigo's stance as he stands. Since he pivots off the left foot, he ends up at a 45-degree angle from Phillipe's body.

5 Rodrigo applies pressure on Phillipe by bracing his right hand on Phillipe's chest and leaning forward. From here he can deliver a series of left punches to the face.

6 To prevent Rodrigo from doing damage with the punches, Phillipe brings his knees in to try to create distance and block the strikes. Rodrigo takes advantage of the counter by taking short steps forward. He forces his hips forward, driving his right thigh against Phillipe's left thigh.

7 Once his hips are over and past Phillipe's hips, Rodrigo grabs Phillipe's left ankle and throws it to his own left side, taking away the obstacle.

8 At this point, Rodrigo would normally try to get his knee on Phillipe's stomach, and then deliver some punches. He also could get across-side to control the pass. Phillipe, however, reacts quickly, and starts to turn turtle by rolling to his own right.

9 Rodrigo cocks his right leg and kicks Phillipe's face.

NHB guard pass to taking the back

A good alternative for the guard pass when the opponent rolls over is taking the back. In the same motion as before, Phillipe turns to all fours as Rodrigo passes the guard, but rather than delivering a kick to the face, Rodrigo opts for taking the back. We pick up the position from the moment that Phillipe begins to turn turtle.

1 Rodrigo has passed Phillipe's guard. As Rodrigo attempts to place his knee on Phillipe's stomach, Phillipe blocks the knee and turns to all fours.

2 Rodrigo immediately drops his body on top of Phillipe. He plants his right hand on the mat near Phillipe's head. His right leg is bent, with the thigh near the mat and the foot ready to hook Phillipe's right leg. Rodrigo's left arm wraps around Phillipe's chest, as his left knee presses down on Phillipe's buttocks.

2 **Reverse angle** Notice how Rodrigo braces off his right arm, keeping his hips slightly off the mat for quicker movement. The right leg is bent, with the thigh parallel to the ground.

3 With his right foot hooking Phillipe's right leg, Rodrigo loops his left foot and hooks Phillipe's left thigh. Rodrigo's left hand grabs Phillipe's right wrist for total control of the position.

4 Rodrigo changes his left hand grip from Phillipe's right wrist to the left one. Rodrigo extends his left leg and pulls Phillipe's left arm back, taking away his brace and forcing Phillipe to the ground. From this position, he can deliver strikes to Phillipe's face. Note: in many events, strikes to the spine and the back of the head are illegal. In order to strike the opponent's face, force his chest flat on the mat, causing his head to turn to one side and allowing access to his face.

Guard pass to footlock

When facing someone with a very good guard, you can spend an inordinate amount of time and energy getting nowhere. Additionally, you are exposed to dangerous heel kicks to the face. One good way to induce fear and have the defender become less aggressive with his feet is to attack with a footlock.

1 Rodrigo is trying to pass Phillipe's guard. He has his right knee up, between Phillipe's legs, and is trying to pass with his knee by sliding it over Phillipe's leg.

2 Phillipe counters with both hands, blocking Rodrigo's knee. Rodrigo has each of his hands on Phillipe's knees, as he tries to push them away to help the pass. Instead of fighting for the pass, Rodrigo decides to attack; he pivots his left leg in, and starts to lean to the left.

3 Rodrigo needs to keep his right knee between Phillipe's legs, blocking him from coming up and countering the foot lock. He holds the top of Phillipe's left knee with his right hand to control the fall and to prevent Phillipe from circling the leg in between Rodrigo's leg, where he can come up and counter the foot lock. Rodrigo wraps his left arm around Phillipe's right ankle as he continues to fall to the mat. Notice that Rodrigo has circled his left foot all the way forward, and he keeps his right knee between Phillipe's legs, to prevent him from coming forward on top of Rodrigo.

4 Rodrigo continues to lean back, as he slides his left arm grip toward the end of Phillipe's leg under the Achilles tendon. He makes sure he traps Phillipe's right foot with his armpit. Rodrigo uses his right hand to grab under his left hand. He also wraps his left leg around Phillipe's right leg, until his foot pushes against Phillipe's stomach. This prevents Phillipe from sitting up to defend the footlock. Rodrigo makes sure he doesn't allow his foot to go too far, and cross in front of Phillipe's stomach. Otherwise, Phillipe can counter with a footlock of his own. Notice that Rodrigo brings his knees together, locking Phillipe's right leg between them. This makes it even more difficult for Phillipe to counter the lock. Rodrigo applies the full pressure by arching his torso back, extending Phillipe's right foot around the ankle.

4 Detail Notice Rodrigo's right hand grip, which is cupped around the left, grabbing under it so he can pull the hand up and apply pressure on Phillipe's Achilles tendon. His forearm adds more pressure to the footlock. Also, notice how Rodrigo's left arm is tightly wrapped around Phillipe's ankle, as close to the foot as possible. In order to apply the most pressure, it is very important to pivot the foot around the ankle. The further up the arm is, the less pressure the footlock will have. Rodrigo uses this alternate grip, instead of the traditional footlock grip, because gloves prevent him from easily executing the traditional grip.

Punching from inside the guard 1

Punches from inside the guard are very common in NHB. Some fighters (especially wrestlers) actually prefer to stay inside and punch in what is called the "ground-n-pound," while jiu-jitsu practitioners use the strikes as a means to open the guard. Since that is such a common occurrence, and because current NHB rules mandate gloves, many times the opponent will hold your gloves, making it difficult for you to punch him from inside the guard. In this case, Phillipe holds the hand across from him (right hand holding the opponent's right hand), but it can work either way, as technique 58 demonstrates. Here, Rodrigo shows one of the ways to strike from the guard.

1 Rodrigo is inside Phillipe's guard, with his hands cupping Phillipe's biceps.

2 Rodrigo creates the necessary space to deliver a punch by raising his torso. Sensing the danger, Phillipe holds Rodrigo's right glove with his right hand. The gloves give Phillipe extra grip, as opposed to just grabbing Rodrigo's wrist, making it more difficult for Rodrigo to free his hand.

3 Rodrigo shifts the control by using his right hand to grip and pull on Phillipe's right wrist. This turns Phillipe to his left and exposes the right side of his face.

4 While still controlling Phillipe's right hand, Rodrigo cocks his left hand and drops a punch on the right side of Phillipe's face.

Punching from inside the guard 2

A variation of the situation in technique 57 is for the opponent to hold the glove on the same side of the body (for example, right hand holds the left hand). In this case, Rodrigo uses the same principle as before to deliver his punches. Pushing Phillipe's arm across his chest makes it more difficult for Phillipe to defend. Since he blocks the left arm, Phillipe is already expecting a right-hand punch from Rodrigo and is ready to block it. So Rodrigo changes the attack. If you are fighting against a much stronger person, it may be difficult to knock him out from the guard, so the punches are used as a diversion for other action, such as standing up to pass the guard. Notice that Rodrigo can either punch or deliver an elbow if elbows are allowed.

1 Phillipe traps Rodrigo's left hand with his right arm by hooking Rodrigo's glove with the nook of his right elbow and pressing his arm to his chest.

2 Rodrigo uses his right hand to grab the top of Phillipe's right hand. He then twists Phillipe's hand while pulling his arm across, which creates a slight space between the elbow and the body.

3 Detail Notice how Rodrigo grabs Phillipe's hand: his fingers cup the top of Phillipe's hand, gripping over the thumb. This gives Rodrigo great leverage to twist and force Phillipe's hand to turn.

3 Rodrigo continues to pull Phillipe's right hand, thus turning Phillipe to his own left and further opening the gap between Phillipe's arm and his chest. This exposes the right side of Phillipe's face. Rodrigo then raises his left elbow to free Phillipe's left hand from the space created by step 2.

4 Rodrigo cocks his left hand and drops a solid punch to the right side of Phillipe's face.

Open-guard pass

It is quite common for the person on the bottom to maintain an open guard with at least one foot pushing the hip of the attacker in order to take away the striking power. In this case, if Rodrigo strikes, Phillipe will simply push off with his right leg and get enough distance to render Rodrigo's punches ineffective. Since this is such a common counter to the strikes, it also presents a good opportunity to pass afterward.

1 Rodrigo has been throwing strikes from his position in Phillipe's guard. Phillipe counters by opening the guard and placing his right foot on Rodrigo's hip. At the same time, he keeps his left leg draped over Rodrigo's back.

2 Rodrigo puts his weight on his hands and raises his hips, while bringing his right leg in toward the center of Phillipe's legs. He lowers his left elbow to lock Phillipe's leg, which prevents Phillipe from bringing the leg up and following the move.

3 Bracing his arms and right knee, Rodrigo loops his left leg back and over Phillipe's right foot. Notice that Rodrigo has to do a big loop: first he must go back to release the pressure from Phillipe's right foot; then he loops his left leg over Phillipe's right foot, so that his thigh hooks over the shin.

4 Rodrigo slides his body up on Phillipe's chest, and hooks his right arm under Phillipe's left arm. At the same time, he uses his left hand to push down on Phillipe's right knee, forcing Phillipe's leg down, while he also steps out wide with his left foot to make a good base.

4 **Reverse angle Incorrect** Notice the incorrect way for Rodrigo to control Phillipe. Here, his right arm hugs Phillipe's head, instead of hooking under Phillipe's left arm. Phillipe can easily go to Rodrigo's back by sliding his hips to his own left.

4 **Reverse angle Correct** Here Rodrigo illustrates the correct way to control. With his right arm under Phillipe's left arm, Rodrigo presses his shoulder against Phillipe's chest. This keeps Phillipe flat on the mat.

5 Rodrigo slides his right knee over Phillipe's right thigh (which is on the ground), while leaving his right foot hooked over Phillipe's thigh. This prevents Phillipe from trapping the foot for the half-guard. At the same time, Rodrigo pulls Phillipe's right arm with his left hand, which keeps Phillipe's back flat on the ground. For this pass to work, it is extremely important for Rodrigo to pull Phillipe's right arm, and to keep Phillipe flat; otherwise, Phillipe can turn toward Rodrigo and replace the guard.

6 Once in firm control over Phillipe, and having established good base, Rodrigo drives his hips forward. He releases his right foot hook and slides his leg forward for the guard pass. Notice how Rodrigo maintains his weight on Phillipe's chest while pulling Phillipe's left arm, to keep Phillipe pinned and flat on the mat.

Guard pass: knee bar (leg inside)

Many times in an NHB match a quick submission is the best option. If you are fighting against a fighter with a very good guard that is difficult to pass, you can expend a lot of energy while your opponent rests and even delivers some kicks. One of the best options, not only for a submission but also to increase the opponent's sense of vulnerability, is to go for the knee bar from the guard pass. Even if the knee bar doesn't end the fight, the attack to the leg will make your opponent worry about his leg movements and loosen his guard. Here, Rodrigo demonstrates the knee bar when his left leg is inside Phillipe's right leg. At worst, Rodrigo creates confusion in Phillipe; at best, he gets a submission.

1 Rodrigo is attempting to pass Phillipe's guard. His left knee presses down against Phillipe's right leg, and his right hand hooks around Phillipe's left leg. It is important for Rodrigo to keep Phillipe's leg straight in order for the knee bar to work; therefore he keeps his right hand over Phillipe's knee and pushes his biceps under Phillipe's calf.

2 Rodrigo pivots off the balls of his feet and turns his body to his right. He drives his left knee in, sliding it over Phillipe's hip, as he dives over Phillipe's left leg and plants his left hand on the mat for balance.

3 Using his left hand as a brace, Rodrigo slides his left knee until it touches the mat next to Phillipe's hip. Rodrigo leaves his left foot hooked on Phillipe's hip, to keep him from sliding his hips away. Rodrigo's right hand maintains control over Phillipe's left leg with the grip he has around Phillipe's knee.

4 Still bracing off his left arm, Rodrigo continues rotating his body around Phillipe's left leg. He also leans back, extending the leg.

5 When his back touches the mat, Rodrigo grabs Phillipe's leg with both arms, and fully extends it as he arches back with his torso. He applies the knee bar by thrusting his hips up, forcing them against Phillipe's knee to hyperextend it.

3 **Reverse angle** Notice Rodrigo's left foot, which is hooked on Phillipe's thigh.

4 **Reverse angle** Rodrigo leaves his right leg draped over Phillipe's leg as he slides his hips on the ground, circling Phillipe's leg. Also notice that Rodrigo slides his right arm up to Phillipe's ankle. This keeps the leg straight so the knee bar can work.

5 **Reverse angle** Rodrigo locks his knees tight against Phillipe's left leg, and wraps his left arm over his right, around the leg.

Guard pass: knee bar (leg outside)

This technique is identical to technique 60, except this time Rodrigo has his left leg outside Phillipe's right leg. In this case, Rodrigo makes a slight adjustment in the mechanics of the move. Again Rodrigo makes sure he keeps Phillipe's left leg straight, using his hand on top of the knee and his biceps behind the calf.

1 Rodrigo attempts to pass Phillipe's guard. This time, Phillipe has his right foot hooked behind Rodrigo's left knee.

2 With his right hand, Rodrigo pulls Phillipe's left leg up. With his left hand, he pushes Phillipe's right leg in. This slightly rotates Phillipe, in a counterclockwise motion, around his back. From here, Rodrigo walks to his right to force Phillipe to keep the hook, and then suddenly changes direction, walking to his left, freeing the hook, and getting close to Phillipe's head.

3 Rodrigo circles around Phillipe's left leg. This time, Rodrigo leans forward, while pivoting off the right foot. He then has to step out and around, over Phillipe's head with his left leg, planting his left foot on the outside of Phillipe's left hip. Notice that Rodrigo walks over Phillipe's head, and not over his chest, because otherwise Phillipe can see the attack and will stop Rodrigo's foot.

4 While still holding Phillipe's leg with his right arm, Rodrigo sits down, directly on top of Phillipe's left hip.

5 Rodrigo leans back and locks his left leg over his right foot. He arches his torso back, extending Phillipe's leg, while pushing his hips forward against the knee.

5 Reverse angle Notice Rodrigo's legs and arms. A figure-four is being executed from locking his left leg over his right foot, which traps Phillipe's thigh. At the same time, he wraps his right arm around Phillipe's ankle, with the nook of his elbow trapping it. Meanwhile, Rodrigo's right hand holds his own left shoulder. Rodrigo's left arm goes over his right one, so that his left hand can hold his right elbow, completely securing control over the ankle. If Rodrigo allows any space, Phillipe might be able to spin his leg around, thus removing the proper angle Rodrigo needs to exert pressure against Phillipe's knee.

Guard pass: knee bar (opponent blocks the hip)

Another common counter that occurs in a guard pass is for the opponent to stiff-arm the passer's hip, blocking the path to the pass. In that case, there is an opportunity for a knee bar as well, and Rodrigo demonstrates it here.

1 Rodrigo attempts to pass Phillipe's guard. His left arm is hooked around Phillipe's right leg, with his right hand pinning Phillipe's left knee. Rodrigo passes to Phillipe's right.

2 As Rodrigo steps around to Phillipe's right, and starts to pass and reach across-side, Phillipe blocks Rodrigo's left hip with his right arm. This prevents Rodrigo from moving forward and blocks the pass. Rodrigo then places both hands on the mat as base points, with his left hand next to Phillipe's left hip, and his right hand opposite, by Phillipe's buttocks. It is important for Rodrigo to keep his right hand outside of Phillipe's legs, just behind his buttocks; if he were to leave his right hand inside, Rodrigo would be open to a triangle.

3 Rodrigo leans forward on his arms, using his shoulder to drive Phillipe's right leg towards Phillipe's left.

4 Still bracing off his arms, Rodrigo circles his left leg around Phillipe's head. Notice that as he leans forward, Rodrigo deflects Phillipe's stiff arm with his hips. Also, Rodrigo opens his leg and pivots it—much like a compass, with his left leg straight out. He makes sure that his foot does not touch the ground at any time, until it gets over Phillipe's right leg and ends up between Phillipe's legs. If his heel touched the mat, it would be easier for Phillipe to defend the attack.

5 Rodrigo continues to circle his left leg around Phillipe's torso. As his leg gets close to Phillipe's left leg, Rodrigo lifts his left hand from the mat and starts to sit down on Phillipe's shoulder. Rodrigo readies his left arm to grasp around Phillipe's leg.

6 As Rodrigo's left leg hooks over Phillipe's left thigh, Rodrigo solidly wraps both arms around Phillipe's right leg. When he falls to the mat, he takes Phillipe's right leg with him. Rodrigo then locks his right leg over his left foot and arches his body back, hyperextending Phillipe's knee. Notice that because Rodrigo's body rotated around Phillipe's right leg, Rodrigo ended up at a 90-degree angle to Phillipe's body. This angle is important, as Rodrigo wants to hyperextend Phillipe's knee. To do it correctly, Rodrigo made sure to begin with his hips facing Phillipe's knee, and then he fell to the side, straight back. If he had fallen to Phillipe's right side, or even toward his head, Rodrigo would not have been facing the knee, and the knee bar would not have worked.

6 **Side view** In this side view, you can clearly see the figure-four lock, with Rodrigo's right leg over his left foot, trapping Phillipe's right leg tightly. Also notice Rodrigo's arm grip around Phillipe's ankle: his left arm is wrapped around the ankle, trapping it in the nook of his elbow. Rodrigo's left hand grips his right shoulder, and his right hand grips his left elbow, removing any space. This prevents Phillipe from spinning and rotating his knee away from the pressure. Remember that the leg is a very powerful limb, capable of resisting much more than an arm, so it is important to be tight when applying a knee bar. An opponent will try to escape the lock by twisting, turning, and rotating the knee, all to avoid the direct pressure.

Guard-pass attack: Kimura

In an NHB fight openings may appear quickly and unexpectedly, so make sure you don't think of a position as a recipe but as a train of thought. In this situation, Rodrigo is attempting to pass Phillipe's guard and Phillipe counters by bracing off his right arm, sitting up and trapping Rodrigo's right leg with his legs and left arm. Rodrigo takes advantage of Phillipe's arm bracing back and goes for a Kimura along with the guard pass. This same technique can be used with minor adaptations any time the opponent is bracing off one arm and you are in front of him, be it a guard pass, a half-guard, or even a mount. Keep an open mind and an eye for similar positions so you can use this technique.

1 Rodrigo attempts to pass Phillipe's guard. He has his right leg between Phillipe's legs, and his hands are touching the knees.

2 Phillipe counters by planting and pushing off his right hand, straightening his arm, and sitting up. Phillipe traps Rodrigo's right leg, with his left arm encircling it. His legs are locking the ankle. At this point, Rodrigo has to gain posture. Otherwise, Phillipe can use a variety of sweeps. Therefore, Rodrigo leans forward with his right knee pushing against Phillipe's chest. He also uses his right hand to keep distance.

3 Seeing the opportunity for an attack, Rodrigo bends at the waist, leans forward, and wraps his right arm around Phillipe's right arm, which is braced on the mat.

4 Rodrigo continues to lean forward, until he can grip Phillipe's right wrist with his left hand. From here, he can lock the Kimura around Phillipe's arm, by grabbing his own left wrist with his right hand. Notice that Rodrigo puts the weight of his body on his arms, effectively locking Phillipe's arm to the mat. At this point, Phillipe senses the danger, and concentrates on defense, giving up his sweep attempt. If Phillipe decides to fight for the sweep from this position, Rodrigo can simply either roll over his left shoulder, and apply the Kimura, or crank the arm around clockwise while standing, with the same result.

5 Rodrigo leans forward until he can brace his head on the mat, next to Phillipe's right shoulder.

6 Pushing off his toes, Rodrigo rolls forward on his head and right shoulder—just enough so that he can jump over to Phillipe's left side, first with his right leg, and then his left one. Rodrigo makes sure not to roll completely over his shoulder.

7 After completing the guard pass, Rodrigo still has the Kimura lock on. Notice that his arms are grapevined around Phillipe's right arm. Rodrigo's left elbow is tight against Phillipe's left hip for control. Rodrigo maintains a lot of his body weight on his elbows, which prevents Phillipe from extending his arm in an attempt to escape the submission.

8 Rodrigo switches his hips, so that they face towards Phillipe's head, by stepping out and over Phillipe's head with his right leg. It is important for Rodrigo to lock his right leg on Phillipe's head, which prevents him from either spinning his body to his right, or sitting up, removing the effectiveness of the lock. Rodrigo leans back, raising Phillipe's arm off the mat, and applies the shoulder lock by driving Phillipe's right arm in a clockwise direction, as if wants to touch Phillipe's right hand to his right ear.

Half-guard attack: Kimura

The Kimura is often available from the half-guard, whether you are on the bottom or the top. Because your body position in relation to your opponent is at a sharp angle, his arm is often vulnerable to a Kimura. In this case, Rodrigo starts to pass the half-guard by bracing and keeping Phillipe's hips down while he slides his right leg up and through. Rodrigo delivers short punches to Phillipe's stomach to release the leg grip. When Phillipe uses his left arm to stop Rodrigo's punches, he exposes it to the lock.

1 Rodrigo is on top in Phillipe's half-guard, with his right leg trapped between Phillipe's legs. Phillipe has his left arm in a good defensive position, with his forearm pushing against Rodrigo's throat to create some space. Rodrigo's left arm is around the back of Phillipe's head, and his right arm is around Phillipe's left arm.

2 Rodrigo begins the pass by moving his body back slightly, so that he can bring his right hand back and under Phillipe's left elbow. He wants to push up the elbow with a combination of the right hand and the head.

3 Having removed Phillipe's left forearm from his throat, and pushing it up slightly, Rodrigo now plants his head on the mat next to Phillipe's left triceps, trapping the arm. At this point, Rodrigo uses his right hand to push down on Phillipe's left leg. He also slides his own right leg up so he can free his right knee from Phillipe's legs. Once he is successful in freeing the knee, Rodrigo has the guard pass almost complete, and he can use a variety of methods to pass, such as the inside knee slide, or the outside knee drive. It is important for Rodrigo to have his head up, and as close to Phillipe's head as possible, so Phillipe cannot try a guillotine. By moving his head near Phillipe's head, Rodrigo also opens up the angle and space, so that he can throw punches.

4 Rodrigo throws a few short punches to Phillipe's stomach. He wants to soften up Phillipe's resolve in maintaining the trap on Rodrigo's leg.

5 Phillipe drops his left hand down, in an attempt to block Rodrigo's punches. Rodrigo, still with his head on the mat, doesn't allow Phillipe's arm to come down. He actually pins the arm with his right hand, grabbing Phillipe's left wrist and pushing it down to the mat.

6 Having secured the control over Phillipe's arm, Rodrigo can take his head off the mat and lean to his left, so that he can create the space under Phillipe's arm. Now, his left hand can slide through and lock onto his right wrist, completing the Kimura lock around Phillipe's left arm.

6 Reverse angle Correct Rodrigo makes sure to keep his left leg open for balance.

6 Reverse angle Incorrect If he has his legs close together, Phillipe can bump up and easily roll him over.

7 Rodrigo brings his left leg in, so that his knee is close to Phillipe's body.

8 Rodrigo then raises his torso, pulling Phillipe to his right, so that Rodrigo can crank Phillipe's arm around and force his hand toward his left ear. This secures the Kimura lock, by applying pressure to the shoulder.

Counter to the scissor sweep: footlock

The scissor sweep works well in NHB because of the opponent's ability to control the arms by holding on to the gloves. Rodrigo shows a great counter for the common scissor sweep.

1 Phillipe controls both of Rodrigo's arms by holding onto his gloves. He applies a scissor sweep, by scissoring his legs and tripping Rodrigo's balance. He holds his left leg low, cutting Rodrigo's right knee, and his left leg pushes against the left side of Rodrigo's body.

2 Phillipe continues the sweeping motion as he extends the right leg, forcing Rodrigo to fall to his back. The first thing Rodrigo does is to raise his right leg; this gets his right knee between Phillipe's legs at the hip. Rodrigo does this to stop Phillipe from coming forward over the top. Notice that Rodrigo plants his left foot, and pushes off it in his attempt to fight the reversal.

3 As Rodrigo's right side starts to touch the mat, Rodrigo leans back and rotates his torso in a clockwise motion. At the same time, he starts to slide his right knee between Phillipe's legs.

4 Rodrigo continues to rotate his torso around his right hip, until he is 180 degrees from Phillipe. Rodrigo's right knee and shin block Phillipe from coming forward on top of Rodrigo.

5 Rodrigo leans back as he traps Phillipe's right ankle with his left arm. He wraps his hand around the ankle, and locks his right hand onto his left. He also arches back, extending Phillipe's right foot and applying the footlock. The gloves prevent Rodrigo from using the standard footlock grip with the hand-grabbing shin.

Passing the butterfly guard

The butterfly guard is an effective guard for NHB. With the foot hooks inside, you protect the foot and leg locks. With your head pressed against the opponent's chest, you protect it against strikes. The butterfly guard is useful for sweeps and as a setup for many of the submissions shown previously in this book, so it is important to be able to pass the butterfly guard, as Rodrigo demonstrates here.

1 Phillipe has Rodrigo in his open guard. Having his back on the mat is not a good thing, as he knows that he cannot control Rodrigo, nor exert any pressure for a sweep. Therefore, he sits up and goes for the butterfly guard, with his arms hooking Rodrigo's arms, and his head pushing against Rodrigo's chest, while keeping his hips away.

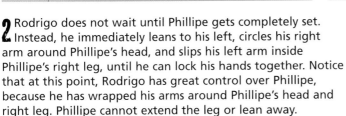

2 Rodrigo does not wait until Phillipe gets completely set. Instead, he immediately leans to his left, circles his right arm around Phillipe's head, and slips his left arm inside Phillipe's right leg, until he can lock his hands together. Notice that at this point, Rodrigo has great control over Phillipe, because he has wrapped his arms around Phillipe's head and right leg. Phillipe cannot extend the leg or lean away.

2 Detail Notice how Rodrigo's right arm wraps around Phillipe's neck. The blade of his forearm presses against Phillipe's throat, exerting a choking pressure. Also notice how Rodrigo's left arm wraps around the right arm, just under Phillipe's right leg. By wrapping around the knee, Rodrigo controls the leg and is able to lock his hands together, with his left hand holding under the right one.

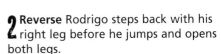

2 Reverse Rodrigo steps back with his right leg before he jumps and opens both legs.

3 Rodrigo jumps back and opens both legs
wide, while pressing down on Phillipe's
head with his chest.

4 He then rotates Phillipe in a clockwise direction, by twisting his shoulders and turning his arms as if he is rocking a baby. He continues turning until he has Phillipe's back on the mat, at which point he releases his hands and reaches across Phillipe's side.

Passing the butterfly guard sweep counter

At times one cannot react quickly enough to apply the previous technique. Here, Rodrigo was either late in applying the pass shown above, or Phillipe was able to reach the advanced stage of the butterfly guard and initiate the sweep motion. Rather than fight the sweep, Rodrigo uses the move to execute a pass. The key to this move is for Rodrigo to maintain his hips parallel to the guard as Phillipe tries to sweep him.

1 Phillipe has reached a great position that sets up a sweep from the butterfly guard. He is sitting up, with the hooks inside Rodrigo's hips, and the right arm hooking Rodrigo's left arm. Phillipe has his left knee back, so he is turned to his left. His left hand controls Rodrigo's right arm, preventing him from opening up and bracing the sweep. Phillipe will initiate the sweep by rocking his body to his left, as if he wants to touch his forehead to the ground near where his left knee is. He kicks and lifts his right leg, bringing Rodrigo with him.

Keep your hips parallel to the ground.

2 As Phillipe attempts the sweep, Rodrigo simply floats up and keeps his hips parallel to the mat. By doing this, Rodrigo negates the sweep, and kills Phillipe's right foot hook control. Rodrigo releases his right arm, circling his hand around Phillipe's left arm. He then plants both hands on the mat for balance.

3 Rodrigo then turns his hips in to his right (clockwise), so as to deflect Phillipe's right leg away, and to allow his left knee to touch the mat. At this point, Rodrigo moves the right hand from the mat to Phillipe's left knee. Notice that Phillipe's right foot no longer controls Rodrigo's legs at all, as his right leg is being pushed down by Rodrigo's hips. Rodrigo circles the right leg over and around Phillipe's right leg, and brings the right knee tight against Phillipe's.

3 **Reverse angle** Notice how Rodrigo moves his hips to loop his right leg around Phillipe's right leg. He raises his hips slightly, so that his left knee slides over Phillipe's left thigh. This allows Rodrigo to maintain pressure over that leg, as he kicks his right leg over Phillipe's right leg.

4 When he reaches across-side position, Rodrigo releases his right hand from Phillipe's left knee and wraps it under Phillipe's left arm, locking his hands for control. Notice that Rodrigo's left arm wraps around the back of Phillipe's neck for a classic NHB side-control hold.

GROUND FIGHTING

Side-Control

Side-control is a very important position in NHB. Because of its stability, side-control is a great position to attack from with strikes and submissions. Since you don't want to lose a position in NHB, the stability of side-control makes it perhaps the safest position from which to attack an opponent in a fight.

In side-control, as in any position, being able to readily use the available arsenal of attacks is a must. By applying pressure and using strikes wisely, you will frustrate your opponent and force him into making a desperate attempt to escape, giving you great chances to finish him.

Because of the stability and control of the position, the key to successfully attacking from side-control is to first maintain the pressure and the position by taking away any space between you and your opponent. Second, control the opponent's head with pressure from your arm and elbow. Third, maintain pressure with your chest on the opponent's chest, keeping him pinned with his back flat on the ground. Fourth, use strikes such as elbows and knees to undermine his resistance and create damage and a sense of doom. Finally, anticipating your opponent's desperate reaction to escape will give you great opportunities to advance your position or to submit him.

Side-control attack: armlock to the far arm (arm trapped out)

Side-control is a great position for an NHB fighter to attack his opponent. From there, Rodrigo can deliver knee strikes to Phillipe's ribs and head, or he can attempt various submissions. In this case, because of the way they ended up, with Phillipe's left arm trapped on the far (right) shoulder, Rodrigo will attack the far arm with an armlock, using a clever controlling grip on Phillipe's upper body.

1 Rodrigo is across Phillipe's side. His left arm is hooked under Phillipe's head, and his shoulder presses against the right side of Phillipe's face, which keeps Phillipe flat on the mat. Rodrigo's right arm is hooked under Phillipe's left arm, exposing the arm. In this case, Phillipe's arm is trapped on Rodrigo's outside (right) shoulder. This may have happened as a consequence of a guard pass, or during a scramble; regardless, Rodrigo sees the arm and is ready to attack. Please note that Rodrigo has his hands clasped together with the palms interlocked.

2 Rodrigo raises his chest slightly off Phillipe and extends his legs, planting his left foot wide. Notice that Rodrigo has raised his left elbow off the mat, forcing Phillipe's head up with it.

3 Rodrigo switches his hips, so they are facing Phillipe, by sliding his right leg through. Making sure his right thigh traps Phillipe's right arm, he ensures that Phillipe cannot escape the elbow to the mat. At the same time, Rodrigo releases the handgrip, and hooks his left hand under the left side of Phillipe's neck, pulling the head up. Rodrigo uses the right arm to trap Phillipe's left arm, by hooking the top of the arm.

4 Rodrigo loops his left leg over Phillipe's head and right arm, landing the foot right next to Phillipe's left ear. At the same time, he leans forward and pushes with his right shoulder to extend Phillipe's left arm. At this point, Rodrigo still pulls up on Phillipe's neck with his left hand. Notice how Rodrigo uses his head to help trap Phillipe's arm as well.

5 Rodrigo slides his left leg under Phillipe's head, and locks his foot over the back of his right knee. This creates a figure-four lock around Phillipe's head and right arm, completely trapping and immobilizing him. Rodrigo puts his left hand on the mat and extends his body, which also extends Phillipe's left arm. Now Rodrigo has the use of two arms to fight against Phillipe's one free arm.

6 Using his left arm, Rodrigo circles his torso to his right and slides his right arm under Phillipe's left elbow. Notice how Rodrigo has locked Phillipe's right arm and head: his left leg is under Phillipe's head, and he has locked his left foot behind his right knee.

7 Rodrigo locks his right hand over his left biceps, and drives his shoulder forward. At the same time, he uses his arms to pull Phillipe's elbow toward his chest for the armlock. Notice how Rodrigo has arched his torso forward to create enough pressure for the lock to work. Had Rodrigo arched his torso back, he would have pushed his belly against Phillipe's elbow, removing any pressure from the lock.

Side-control attack: head-and-arm triangle (arm trapped in)

Another possibility from the same position is for the arm to be trapped on the inside shoulder, between Rodrigo's head and left shoulder. In this case, instead of going for the armlock, Rodrigo prefers to go for the head-and-arm triangle.

1 Rodrigo lies across Phillipe's side, with his left arm hooked under Phillipe's head. Rodrigo's right arm is hooked under Phillipe's left arm, exposing it. In this case, Phillipe's arm is trapped between Rodrigo's head and his inside (left) shoulder.

2 Rodrigo releases the handgrip and places his right elbow on the mat, pressing it tight against Phillipe's body, taking away any space for Phillipe to move his upper body. With his left hand, he reaches around Phillipe's left shoulder and grabs under his armpit. At the same time, Rodrigo uses his head to drive Phillipe's left arm up toward his head.

3 **Alternate view** Rodrigo then braces his right forearm against Phillipe's stomach.

4 Rodrigo places his right hand on Phillipe's left hip, pushes off, and raises his hips. At the same time, he further drives his head up, trapping and forcing Phillipe's arm against his own head. Rodrigo's hand presses down on Phillipe's left hip, both as a brace point to jump over, and also to keep Phillipe from raising the hip and catching Rodrigo's legs as he jumps over.

5 Rodrigo jumps over Phillipe and lands on his left side. Pushing off his left foot, he loops his right leg up high over Phillipe's body. Once it clears Phillipe's legs, Rodrigo follows with the left leg. It is important for Rodrigo to lift his legs as high as he can, so that Phillipe cannot catch them with his legs and trap for the half-guard. Notice that Rodrigo pushes down on his right hand, not only to help him move, but also to keep Phillipe's hips flat on the ground.

6 Rodrigo ends up on Phillipe's left side, with his hips facing forward and his right foot firmly planted out for base. His left knee is positioned slightly back and touching the mat. From this position, Rodrigo has successfully trapped Phillipe's head and arm.

7 Rodrigo locks his left hand over his right biceps, and places the palm of his right hand on Phillipe's forehead. He squares his hips as he brings his right knee in near Phillipe's left shoulder, at the same time applying pressure and driving his torso forward. This pushes Phillipe's arm against his own throat. On the other side, Rodrigo uses his left shoulder to assist with the choke.

7 **Reverse angle** Notice how Rodrigo applies the choking pressure, by using his left arm and shoulder to press on the right side of Phillipe's neck. Rodrigo's head and body force Phillipe's left arm against the left side of Phillipe's neck, as well. It is important for Rodrigo to be at a 45-degree, diagonal angle from Phillipe; if his body were parallel, the pressure would not be as strong. Also, notice that this is a choke, and not a neck crank. When you try this move, check to see if your opponent feels the neck crank; if so, adjust your position. This is a triangle choke, which uses arms rather than legs, so remember to squeeze the choke. Here, Rodrigo does this by using his left arm on one side of the choke, while pressing Phillipe's arm against his own neck on the other side.

Side-control attack: triangle

Another option for attack from side-control is the triangle. Rodrigo chooses the triangle attack when Phillipe's arm is in a good defensive position. Notice that this time Phillipe's arm is not extended, but rather is braced against Rodrigo's throat in a good defensive posture, making it difficult for Rodrigo to attack the right arm. Rodrigo goes for the mount and on Phillipe's reaction he applies the triangle.

1 Rodrigo has side-control on Phillipe. However, Phillipe's left arm is bent with the forearm pressing against Rodrigo's throat, creating a very uncomfortable pressure against Rodrigo's larynx. Phillipe's left arm is in a good, defensive position, while his right arm is trapped between Rodrigo's left leg and the side of his body. Notice that Phillipe's elbow is on the outside.

2 Rodrigo starts his attack by sliding his right knee over Phillipe's stomach. If Phillipe does not block the move, Rodrigo will end up mounted. Rodrigo locks Phillipe's left arm by exerting pressure with his arms.

3 Sensing the impending mount, Phillipe releases the left arm block against the throat, and uses his left hand to block the knee slide and to prevent Rodrigo from mounting.

4 Rodrigo pulls his right arm back, and with his right hand, he locks Phillipe's left wrist, pressing it down against Phillipe's thigh. From this position, Rodrigo has several options: he can go back to the knee-slide mount over the locked hand; he can go for a Kimura attack to the left arm; or he can go for the triangle. He opts for the triangle.

5 Rodrigo leans back, toward his left, and loops his right leg over his right arm, landing with his right foot slightly wide. Notice that as soon as his leg goes over, he has to release the wrist and remove his arm; otherwise, he will stop his own progress.

5 **Top view** Notice how Rodrigo circles his leg over Phillipe's legs and left arm, while maintaining the pressure on the wrist with his right hand. Rodrigo's leg is only partially extended, thus making a shorter route over the legs.

6 Rodrigo leans to his right, sits on Phillipe's chest, and continues to circle his right leg until it locks under Phillipe's neck. At the same time, Rodrigo uses his left hand to pull Phillipe's head up off the mat; this assists in positioning his leg under the neck.

7 Having his right leg curled and tight against Phillipe's neck, Rodrigo locks his left hand to his right shin to secure the grip around Phillipe's neck. Now, Rodrigo must complete the figure-four hold by locking his left leg over his right foot.

8 To do so, Rodrigo rolls over to his right, bringing Phillipe with him. Since Rodrigo's weight is already leaning forward, he uses that to roll them over. Notice that Rodrigo maintains a firm grip around Phillipe's head by grabbing his right shin with his left hand as he rolls.

9 Halfway through the roll, Rodrigo is able to loop his left leg over his right foot, locking the figure-four. Notice that Rodrigo's right foot is tucked in the nook of his left knee.

10 At the end of the roll, Rodrigo has executed the perfect triangle choke, and he applies pressure by closing the knees together, and pulling Phillipe's head in with both hands.

Side-control attack: opponent defends triangle

A very common counter to the triangle is for the opponent to stand up.
Although it is not the preferred way to counter, it is a common reaction, especially from fighters who are not jiu-jitsu experts. Here, Rodrigo is ready for the counter and switches to an armlock.

1 Rodrigo has Phillipe in a triangle choke, but he has not yet completely locked it.

2 Phillipe stands up in order to create some space and counter the choke.

3 Rodrigo maintains control over Phillipe's right hand, with his left hand over the wrist, and he thrusts his hips up and extends his body. Notice that from this position, should Rodrigo be able to swing Phillipe's right hand around his face, he might be able to execute the armlock by pushing Phillipe's wrist toward his left shoulder, and forcing Phillipe's right arm against his left thigh, thereby hyperextending the elbow.

4 Rodrigo pivots his torso as he extends his right arm to reach around Phillipe's left ankle with his right hand. Notice that Rodrigo has maintained the triangle lock in place, although it may have loosened slightly because of the counter. Rodrigo prevents Phillipe from escaping or pulling away by pressing down on the back of Phillipe's neck with his right calf.

The hips must be up for the submission to work.

5 Rodrigo quickly releases the figure-four lock and circles his right leg over Phillipe's head, while extending his hips and driving his calves down against Phillipe's head for the armlock. He makes sure to pull his heel towards his own buttocks in order to maintain pressure on Phillipe's neck, thus preventing him from pulling out.

Side-control attack: knee bar

In a fight, being mounted is one of the last places you want to be. Fighters defend the mount with everything they have. Here, Rodrigo has reached side-control on Phillipe, which is already a bad position for Phillipe. Now Rodrigo tries to advance to the mount and uses Phillipe's reaction to go for the knee bar. Rodrigo begins with the real intention of mounting Phillipe; he only switches to the knee bar when Phillipe applies this counter.

1 Rodrigo is across Phillipe's side. Rodrigo's right arm is under and around Phillipe's left arm, and his left arm is around Phillipe's head. In addition, Rodrigo's shoulder presses against Phillipe's chin, preventing Phillipe from turning into Rodrigo. Rodrigo has locked both hands, with palms facing each other; his knees are in next to Phillipe's torso. This is a classic NHB side-control position.

2 With his right arm, Rodrigo reaches around Phillipe's right leg and grabs over his left thigh. Rodrigo starts to drive Phillipe's right leg across his own body to his left side. If Phillipe allows this to happen, Rodrigo will simply loop his right leg over Phillipe's body and end up with the mount.

3 Phillipe reacts, however, and tries to push in the opposite direction as he straightens his right leg and brings it back to center. At this point, there is a slight stalemate, as Rodrigo blocks Phillipe from executing this movement by locking his right arm firmly around Phillipe's left thigh. Notice that Rodrigo has released his left arm from around Phillipe's head, and has planted it as a brace on the mat near Phillipe's head.

4 With Phillipe's reaction, Rodrigo goes for the submission. By bracing his arms and right knee, Rodrigo circles his left leg around Phillipe's head.

5 As the leg passes over Phillipe's torso, and nears his own left arm, Rodrigo releases his arm from the mat and sits on the right side of Phillipe's ribs. From here, he continues to circle his leg and body around Phillipe's right leg.

6 When his left leg reaches over Phillipe's left leg, Rodrigo leans forward and wraps his right arm around Phillipe's right leg. He also braces on the mat with his left forearm.

7 Rodrigo ends up in a similar position to the other knee-bar techniques. He is on his left side, in the familiar 90-degree angle to Phillipe's body. As he fell, he locked his right leg over his left foot for the figure-four lock around Phillipe's right leg. This has allowed Rodrigo to hyperextend Phillipe's knee.

Side-control attack: punch to armlock

One can never forget that strikes are allowed in NHB matches. The introduction of the strikes in any situation will cause tremendous chaos, allowing for various options to open up. Whereas in a sports jiu-jitsu or submission grappling match the opponent could rest easy with someone across-side and wait for the proper opportunity to escape, in an NHB match the threat of strikes adds urgency. Rodrigo takes advantage of the side-control position to deliver some punches to Phillipe's face. Upon Phillipe's reaction, he simply locks the arm out of the way and continues to deliver the punishment.

1 Rodrigo is across Phillipe's side. Notice not only Rodrigo's proper controlling grip, but also Phillipe's defensive arm posture. Phillipe's right forearm blocks Rodrigo's hips and possible knee strikes; his left forearm, with the hand braced against Rodrigo's left shoulder, pushes against Rodrigo's throat to create some space.

2 Rodrigo quickly switches his base so his hips are facing toward Phillipe's head. He does this by bracing off his elbows and the tips of his toes, lifting his hips, and shooting his right leg toward Phillipe's left shoulder. Rodrigo successfully punches Phillipe's face once when he reaches this position, but Phillipe can see him cock his left arm to deliver a second punch. Phillipe raises the right arm to intercept the strike.

3 Rodrigo grabs Phillipe's right wrist with the left hand, and pushes Phillipe's arm out and over his right leg. At this point, Rodrigo can continue to push down on Phillipe's right wrist, forcing the arm down and hyperextending the elbow.

4 Instead, however, he clears the block by looping his left leg over Phillipe's right arm, and trapping it between his legs. Notice that Rodrigo has locked his left foot around his right calf, and presses his knees together to prevent Phillipe from pulling his arm away.

5 Rodrigo cocks his left arm, and Phillipe blocks the right side of his face with his left hand, attempting to protect himself from Rodrigo's punch.

6 Rodrigo loops the punch over Phillipe's left hand, striking over his arm to his face. Had Rodrigo tried to deliver a straight punch, it would have been blocked by Phillipe's left hand.

Side-control attack: punch to knee strikes

Many times when you start punching, the opponent is able to turn into you and use his other arm (left arm) to block his face from punches. Faced with that situation here, Rodrigo immediately switches to knee strikes.

1 Rodrigo loops a punch over Phillipe's arm, striking him.

2 Phillipe turns into Rodrigo, and uses his left arm to block Rodrigo's punches. Rodrigo releases the leg grip on Phillipe's right arm, and with his left hand grabs the back of Phillipe's head, to keep it from moving back. Rodrigo's right arm grabs Phillipe's back. Keeping his elbow firm on the mat prevents Phillipe from escaping his torso.

3 Rodrigo loops his left thigh over Phillipe's right hand, as he pulls Phillipe's head with his right hand.

4 Rodrigo then strikes Phillipe's face. Notice that if Rodrigo were not controlling Phillipe's head with his left hand, Phillipe would be able to bob, dodging some of the knee strikes.

5 To block the knee strikes, Phillipe uses his right forearm against Rodrigo's left thigh. Rodrigo forces his left knee against Phillipe's arm, provoking another reaction from Phillipe.

6 Before he loops it over Phillipe's forearm again, Rodrigo cocks his left leg all the way back, releasing the block created by Phillipe's right forearm. Rodrigo loops his left leg over and strikes Phillipe's face with his knee.

Side-control attack: knee strikes to clock choke

In this continuation of the same sequence of positions, once Phillipe starts being hit by Rodrigo's knees, he will struggle even more to avoid further damage. He has two options. The first is to somehow turn to his left. This is the more difficult option, since Rodrigo has control over his left shoulder and is keeping him flat on the ground. However, even if he could do that, he would simply be giving up his back to Rodrigo. Rodrigo could easily place hooks and go for a rear naked choke. The other and more common option is for Phillipe to turn his body to his right, into Rodrigo's, and turn turtle. In that case, Rodrigo uses this technique to apply a devastating clock choke. We pick up from technique 74, step 6.

1 Rodrigo delivers another knee strike to Phillipe's face.

3 Phillipe continues to turn to his right. His right hand is placed in front of the left side of his face, in order to block Rodrigo's punches. Rodrigo continues to punch as Phillipe turns. Notice Rodrigo's new stance: with his right hand on the ground for support, and his left foot firmly planted on the mat with the knee up, Rodrigo pushes off that leg to maintain pressure on Phillipe's back. This controls whether and how fast he can rotate. Rodrigo does not want Phillipe to be able to turn quickly to all fours, so he pushes down on Phillipe's torso with his chest, which slows him down. Rodrigo's right knee is inside, between Phillipe's left knee and left arm, and Rodrigo is in a perfect three-point stance. With this base, he is ready to quickly react to any movement Phillipe may initiate.

2 Not wanting to continue in a dire situation, Phillipe explodes, attempting to escape. Pushing off his left leg, Phillipe bridges and turns to his right, using both arms in front of the face to block Rodrigo's knee. Rodrigo continues the assault as Phillipe turns and delivers some punches to Phillipe's head. Notice that Rodrigo changes his body position, in order to follow Phillipe's escape. He braces his right hand on the mat, and steps back with his left foot. He pushes off his left foot, which allows him to raise his hips and bring his right leg back under him. This allows his knee to touch the mat.

4 As Phillipe attempts to get up, Rodrigo continues to punch the side of his face. This forces Phillipe to use his right hand to block the punches. Notice Rodrigo's right knee position; it is forward and next to Phillipe's left arm, blocking the arm from coming back.

5 Taking advantage of Phillipe's right arm position (which is there to block the punches), Rodrigo slides his right arm around Phillipe's neck. When his right hand reaches the other side of Phillipe's neck, Rodrigo locks his left hand onto his right wrist for a choke. Once he locks the hands, Rodrigo starts to slide the right knee forward, while making sure he maintains the pressure of his body on Phillipe's back.

6 Rodrigo applies the full-clock choke by pulling his right forearm with his left arm, and cinching the choke. At the same time, he slides his right leg forward and extends it, so that his hips are forward and his weight is on the side of the chest. From here, he applies pressure to the top of Phillipe's neck, pushing it down against the choking forearm. Notice that, for maximum pressure, Rodrigo's body is at approximately 90 degrees to Phillipe's body, with his right leg in a straight line with Phillipe's head.

6 Incorrect This is the incorrect way to apply the choke. Instead of having his hips up, and the weight off his body and on the back of Phillipe's neck, Rodrigo has his hips and right leg past the proper point. It is important for Rodrigo not to go too far with his body, as he does here. Otherwise, not only does he lose the pressure of the choke, but he is also completely out of balance. His right foot cannot pass beyond the line of Phillipe's head, and he cannot put his buttocks on the ground. This transfers weight to the ground, instead of onto Phillipe's neck.

Side-control counter: how to block the low knee strike

Delivering punishment is the desired situation in any fight, however there are times when you may end up in a bad situation and being able to properly defend and bring the situation to a safe environment may save your match. One common attack from side-control is the low knee strike. Being able to quickly and effectively block it is a must. Here Rodrigo demonstrates the block. He is aware that the knee strike is one of the best striking options and that he needs to react as soon as he feels his opponent's body move. Notice that for Phillipe to deliver the knee strike, he has to create some space between his chest and Rodrigo's chest, and also to turn his body slightly to his left, raising the right shoulder. This is the sign to Rodrigo that the knees are coming. The distance that Rodrigo has to move his knee to block is a lot shorter than the distance Phillipe has to move his knee to strike. Advantage: Rodrigo.

1 Phillipe is in side-control, with Rodrigo on the bottom. He cocks his right (low) leg to deliver a knee strike to Rodrigo's midsection. Notice that in order to deliver a solid knee strike, Phillipe has to create some distance between himself and Rodrigo by raising his torso away. Notice Rodrigo's great defensive arm posture. His right arm is bent with the elbow on the ground, his forearm is blocking the high knee strike, and his left forearm is pressing against Phillipe's throat. This creates space between his and Phillipe's chest.

2 As soon as he feels Phillipe's intentions, Rodrigo steps out slightly with his left foot and pushes off, escaping his hips as far to his left as possible. He also turns his body into Phillipe, while extending his arms to distance himself even more from Phillipe.

3 Rodrigo quickly brings his right knee in front of Phillipe's right leg, blocking the strike with his shin. From this point, Rodrigo can work on replacing the guard, as well as bringing his hips in front of Phillipe's hips in order to square himself with Phillipe.

Side-control attack: Kimura

Side-control is a very stable position, therefore it is very desirable during an NHB match. Keep in mind that, more so than in sports jiu-jitsu or submission grappling, in NHB any forward progress is very precious and needs to be protected. The last thing you want to do in an NHB fight is to relinquish a good position, so the side-control became a favorite position for submission attacks and strikes. In this technique, Rodrigo attacks Phillipe's outside arm with a Kimura. Notice that Rodrigo starts the attack much in the same way as he would attempt an armlock, but since Phillipe bends the arm down, it is already at the perfect angle for a Kimura.

1 Rodrigo is across Phillipe's side. Phillipe's left arm is bent and pushing against Rodrigo's face to create some space. Rodrigo takes advantage of that, and goes for a Kimura. With his left arm, Rodrigo encircles Phillipe's left arm.

2 Rodrigo springs off his legs with his toes on the mat, and starts to walk to his left. As Rodrigo gets to the north-south position, Phillipe begins to counter by trying to remove his arm from danger. Because Rodrigo's left arm encircles Phillipe's left arm, Phillipe cannot simply pull it out to defend; he decides to bend it and bring it down instead.

3 With his right hand Rodrigo grabs Phillipe's left wrist, and locks his left hand on his own right wrist, locking the perfect Kimura control.

3 Reverse Notice that Rodrigo's left arm is wrapped around Phillipe's left arm, and his left hand locks onto his right wrist. At the same time, his right hand is locked onto Phillipe's left wrist. Also notice Rodrigo's body position: his chest is pressing against Phillipe's left shoulder, to keep him from moving his body to the left and flattening on the mat to counter the Kimura. At this point, Rodrigo can either go for the Kimura or the armlock. In an NHB match, the Kimura is a safer alternative, as you do not end up on the bottom if you fail the submission (or, you maintain the top position even if the submission fails).

4 In full control over Phillipe's arm, Rodrigo raises his torso and steps out with the left leg, while using his right leg to trap Phillipe's right arm. This prevents Phillipe from locking his hands together and defending the Kimura. Rodrigo pulls Phillipe's arm to his own right, away from Phillipe's body, to create space.

4 Reverse Notice how Rodrigo steps over Phillipe's right arm with his right leg, placing the knee just over the arm, and leaving the foot hook on the opposite side. This prevents Phillipe from locking his hands, and helps with the leverage for the Kimura.

5 Rodrigo brings Phillipe's arm back to his left, cranking the Kimura and applying torque to Phillipe's left shoulder. Notice that the direction of the submission is for Rodrigo to direct Phillipe's hand counterclockwise, as if he wants to touch Phillipe's hand to his left ear.

Side-control attack: cervical lock

Another very effective attack from side-control is the cervical lock. Because it involves attacking the spine, the cervical lock may be illegal in certain events. Make sure you know the rules.

1 Rodrigo has Phillipe in side-control.

2 Rodrigo releases his right hand from his left, and circles it in front of Phillipe's left biceps. At the same time, he starts to lean forward, until he can lock his hands again. Once he locks the hands together, Rodrigo starts to lean to his right side. Notice that Rodrigo's right elbow is firm on the ground, with a lot of his body weight on it. As Rodrigo leans to his right, he brings his left arm up and forces Phillipe's head up off the mat.

3 Rodrigo springs up, as he steps out with his left leg and continues to lean to his right. This applies even more pressure on Phillipe's neck. Notice that Rodrigo's right elbow is still on the mat, and Rodrigo uses it as a brace. Rodrigo's right elbow slides out, forcing Phillipe's left arm open and allowing Rodrigo to reach and grab under Phillipe's armpit (in the next step).

4 Rodrigo continues leaning forward and to his right, forcing Phillipe's head up. Once he has Phillipe's head off the mat enough, Rodrigo reaches with his left hand and locks it in Phillipe's left armpit. Rodrigo drives his left knuckles to the mat to add pressure.

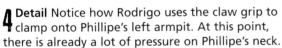

4 Detail Notice how Rodrigo uses the claw grip to clamp onto Phillipe's left armpit. At this point, there is already a lot of pressure on Phillipe's neck.

5 Rodrigo uses his right hand to pull Phillipe's head forward even more, applying additional pressure on the neck, and finishing the submission. Notice that it is very important for Rodrigo to keep Phillipe's back on the ground, so that pressure is maintained on the neck. If Rodrigo allows Phillipe's back to come off the ground, as if he were sitting up, pressure on the neck would be reduced tremendously. The direction of the pressure is for Rodrigo to pull Phillipe's head into his own chest.

Side-control attack: choke

Another option from side-control is the choke. At times, when you go for the neck crank, your opponent quickly reacts by forcing his head back to the ground. In this case—or if the cervical hold in technique 78 is illegal, or another attack weapon is desired—this choke is always available. We pick up the attack from technique 78, step 2.

1 Rodrigo has his hands clasped together, right hand over left, with his right elbow on the ground, and his left arm around the back of Phillipe's neck, forcing it up. At this point, he can easily go for the cervical lock, or use this choke. Phillipe senses the attack, and defends it by pushing his head down and toward the mat. This makes the cervical hold a more difficult option for Rodrigo.

2 Rodrigo leans back, and circles his right elbow on top of Phillipe's chest, driving his right forearm around toward Phillipe's throat. It is very important for Rodrigo to slide the elbow and the forearm on Phillipe's chest; otherwise, he will not lock it under Phillipe's chin for the choke.

3 Rodrigo applies the choke on Phillipe by continuing to bring his right arm back, and driving his left arm forward, as if he wanted to touch his elbows together. Notice that Rodrigo spins his torso to his right, as he brings his arms and elbows together.

3 Detail Notice Rodrigo's hands, which are clasped with the palms together. Also, notice how Rodrigo uses the back blade of his right forearm against Phillipe's throat, to create maximum pressure. It is a common mistake to try to choke with the side of the arm instead of the back blade; this is why it is important to lock the hands in the proper way. When you try this move, always keep the palm facing up on the hand that is in front of the neck. This hand also needs to be under the other hand; otherwise, you will use the side of the forearm to choke. The pressure comes from putting the right elbow to the ground, pulling the left elbow up, and lifting the head against the blade of the right forearm.

Side-control attack: armlock

A common way for an opponent to attempt to escape from side-control is to use both arms to push away the person on top. Since it is difficult to push away someone bigger than you, this usually happens as the person on top moves to adjust a position or to initiate an attack. A similar situation also occurs at the end of the guard pass when the passer is fighting to establish side-control and the defender is pushing to block. Regardless of how the situation occurs, the stiff arm on the hips allows for the armlock that Rodrigo demonstrates here.

1 Phillipe's right arm is pushing Rodrigo's left hip away, and his left arm is pushing Rodrigo's right shoulder. Sensing that he is losing ground, and rather than fighting the pressure, Rodrigo changes to an armlock. He starts by locking Phillipe's right elbow with his left hand, and pulling it up. Rodrigo does not want Phillipe to counter the attack by pulling his arm away, or by bending the elbow.

2 Bracing off his right arm, Rodrigo pulls up on Phillipe's elbow, releasing the hand from his hips and allowing him to move his hips closer to Phillipe's right elbow, as he traps Phillipe's right arm under his left armpit.

3 Bracing off his right hand and left foot, Rodrigo raises his hips high, so he can get his right knee above Phillipe's stomach. Rodrigo pushes off his right arm, and raises his torso, as if he were going to put his knee on Phillipe's stomach. However, instead, he puts his knee inside Phillipe's armpit, while controlling Phillipe's right triceps with his left hand.

4 Rodrigo drives his right knee forward, so that his right shin pushes against Phillipe's right armpit. At this point, Rodrigo starts to lean back and to sit on the mat. Notice that Phillipe's right arm is in a very vulnerable position, with the wrist locked by Rodrigo's left armpit, and the elbow locked by Rodrigo's left hand and left hip. The arm is so extended that any slight lean by Rodrigo will pop the elbow joint.

5 Rodrigo completes the armlock by bringing his left leg around, so that his foot is next to Phillipe's head. He brings both knees together, reducing any space around Phillipe's right elbow. As he leans back, Phillipe has to submit or have his elbow damaged. If he needs to, Rodrigo can shoot his hips upward, in case his opponent has extremely flexible arms. When you practice this move, be very careful; your partner's arm is so extended in this position that any leaning back or abrupt movement will pop the elbow.

Side-control attack: shoulder lock

A great option from side-control is this clever shoulder lock to the near arm. In this case, Rodrigo has his hips switched so they are facing towards Phillipe's head with the left arm controlling Phillipe's right arm. This is a common immobilization position usually used in transition, as Rodrigo cannot deliver many strikes from here. Since it is a relatively "safe" position for the defender, he normally relaxes. Rodrigo takes advantage of that and attacks the near arm with a shoulder lock similar to the "Americana," except using the legs to pressure the lock.

1 Rodrigo has side-control on Phillipe, with his hips facing up toward Phillipe's head, and his left arm pulling on Phillipe's right arm. Notice that Rodrigo's left foot is planted on the mat, with the knee up. He is ready to spring his body into action, and to react to any attempts by Phillipe to escape the position. Rodrigo's right arm underhooks Phillipe's left arm, with his hand holding the shoulder.

2 Phillipe twists his right arm around to escape the control, and circles his hand around the outside of Rodrigo's elbow.

3 As Phillipe's hand gets near his own head, Rodrigo has to react or risk losing control of the arm, because Phillipe can continue with the motion, and release the arm from under Rodrigo's right-hand control. Rodrigo quickly changes his grip from Phillipe's triceps to the right wrist. He pushes it down, while at the same time he kicks his right leg forward.

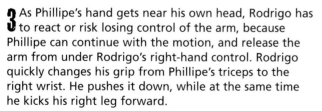

4 Rodrigo circles his right leg over Phillipe's right hand, and presses down on it. At this point, Rodrigo's left hand can release Phillipe's wrist. Rodrigo brings his right heel back and close to his buttocks. Notice how Phillipe's right arm is in a precarious position, with the wrist trapped under Rodrigo's right ankle, and the elbow propped against the thigh.

5 Rodrigo loops his left leg over his right foot, locking the figure-four around Phillipe's right arm. He then circles his left arm around Phillipe's head until it reaches his own right arm, locks his hands, and pulls up on Phillipe's head. He also applies pressure on Phillipe's shoulder, by turning his hips in a counterclockwise direction and pushing Phillipe's elbow forward, while pulling his hand back with the legs torquing Phillipe's shoulder.

Side-control escape counter: guillotine

One of the most effective ways to escape from side-control is for a fighter to bridge up into his opponent, drive his top arm forward, and turn to his knees, ending up facing his opponent on all fours, or even better grabbing the opponent's leg so he can reverse him. This often occurs as the top fighter transitions to a submission, or if he doesn't have the proper weight on the position yet, because he hasn't fully established side-control. Rodrigo demonstrates a very effective counter to the escape.

1 Rodrigo has side-control on Phillipe. Phillipe bridges and turns to his right, into Rodrigo, as he attempts to escape the side-control. Rodrigo normally would try to press his chest down, forcing Phillipe's right shoulder back down until he has his back flat on the mat, however this time he is late and cannot do that, perhaps because he was transitioning to a submission. Regardless, Rodrigo counters by wrapping his right arm around Phillipe's right arm, right near the armpit, as he steps out with his right foot. He makes sure that his knee points up, and that the foot is outside of Phillipe's legs.

2 As Phillipe continues to turn to his knees, Rodrigo sits back on the mat and wraps the left arm around Phillipe's neck. He presses the blade of his forearm against Phillipe's throat until he can lock his hands together for the guillotine hold. Notice that Rodrigo's right leg is already outside of Phillipe's left leg, and that his left leg is bent, with the knee pointing out. This allows him to easily circle the leg around Phillipe's right arm. Notice that since Phillipe was turning to his right, his right arm has the longest path to reach out, and it ends up trapped by Rodrigo's leg.

3 After locking the guillotine hold around Phillipe's left arm and neck, Rodrigo leans back until his back touches the mat. He then wraps his left leg over Phillipe's right arm, fully trapping it. Rodrigo locks his feet together, with the left one over the right, for closed guard. Notice Phillipe's predicament: his right arm is trapped by Rodrigo's left leg, and his left arm is trapped by Rodrigo's right arm in the guillotine. Rodrigo applies choking pressure by leaning back and turning his torso to his right. He then pulls the arms tight, forcing his left forearm against Phillipe's throat for the choke.

3 Detail Notice how Rodrigo's left leg locks over Phillipe's right shoulder, preventing him from pulling the arm out or using it in any way to defend the choke.

GROUND FIGHTING

Mount and Back Attacks

Attaining the mount or the back in a fight is one of the best positions you can have. In NHB, you should be able to finish the fight from there with strikes. But make sure you maintain the mount! Some fighters are so eager to submit an opponent that they forget to maintain position and end up losing the mount. By maintaining the mount, you force your opponent to open up, giving you opportunities for submissions. Once your opponent feels trapped, he will try desperate things, exposing himself to submissions. Once you are confident of your ability to maintain the position, you can be a lot more deliberate about going for submissions; take your time and wait for the right opportunities.

Taking the back is even better than the mount. You are behind the opponent, you can't be attacked, and you have many options for strikes and submissions. Your opponent is not even capable of seeing what you have coming. As with the mount, step one is to maintain the position, step two is to go for the submission.

Mounted attack: punch to key-lock

Many good things happen when the opponent has to worry about protecting himself from submissions and strikes, especially when he is mounted. In this case, Rodrigo takes advantage of Phillipe's attempt to block his punches and goes for a key-lock. The key to this technique is the fact that Phillipe's arm is bent as it is driven up. Should the arm be straight, Rodrigo will go for the head-and-arm triangle, as explained in technique 84.

1 Rodrigo is mounted on Phillipe, with his left arm wrapped around Phillipe's head. Rodrigo has his right arm free to punch Phillipe's face. Phillipe is aware of this, and uses his left arm to block Rodrigo's punches. Rodrigo applies pressure with his right arm, fighting Phillipe's defense.

2 Sensing Phillipe's upward pressure with the left hand, Rodrigo quickly pulls his right arm back, thereby releasing Phillipe's block and overextending Phillipe's left arm.

3 Rodrigo circles his right arm back in, trapping Phillipe's left arm as Rodrigo crawls forward with his right hand.

4 Rodrigo continues to crawl forward with his right hand, further trapping Phillipe's left arm and forcing it upward toward his head. As Rodrigo forces Phillipe's arm up, Phillipe tries to push it back down. This is the moment to change and go for the key-lock. Notice that Phillipe's left arm is bent; that is Rodrigo's sign to go for the key-lock.

5 Once Phillipe's left hand is almost over his head, Rodrigo traps his left wrist with his left hand. Notice that Rodrigo's grip has all five fingers on the same side, in a claw-type grasp. By using all the fingers in this way, rather than the more common position with four fingers on one side and the thumb on the other, Rodrigo has much more controlling power.

6 Once in control of the wrist, Rodrigo slides his left arm around from under Phillipe's head. He then slides his right hand into the space under Phillipe's left arm, near the elbow, until his right hand can grab his own left wrist.

7 Once he has the key-lock in place, Rodrigo applies pressure on Phillipe's shoulder by sliding Phillipe's left hand down towards Rodrigo's right knee. He also lifts the right elbow, torquing Phillipe's arm around his shoulder. It is important for Rodrigo to keep Phillipe's hand on the mat at all times. If Phillipe's hand rises off the mat, it will take a lot more turning to achieve the same pressure. Some people have a much greater range of motion in their shoulders than others, making it very difficult to submit them. When you try this move, remember that the more you bring the hand down toward the knee, the more torque you will apply. Also, make sure you keep the hand as close to the body as possible; the farther out the hand is, the less pressure you can apply.

Mounted attack: head-and-arm triangle

Another option from the mount is the head-and-arm triangle. As stated in technique 83, the deciding factor as to which technique to use is Phillipe's arm position. If his arm is bent, Rodrigo can easily reach the wrist with his hand that is wrapped around the head and go for the key-lock. If the arm is straight, Rodrigo cannot reach the wrist with his hand, so he must choose the head-and-arm triangle. We pick up the technique from step 83.4, when Rodrigo has already trapped Phillipe's arm and is crawling his right hand forward, driving the arm over Phillipe's head.

1 Rodrigo crawls his hand on the mat, driving Phillipe's left arm around toward his own head. In this case, Phillipe's arm is straight, making it difficult for Rodrigo to apply the key-lock, and calling for the head-and-arm triangle. As Phillipe's arm hits the side of his own head, Rodrigo reaches with his left arm, which is still wrapped around Phillipe's head, and grabs the outside of the triceps. This exchanges the control of the arm from the right arm to the left hand.

2 Rodrigo uses his right hand to push Phillipe's left arm across and over his face, locking the arm in place with his own head.

3 Notice that Rodrigo drives his head down against Phillipe's left arm, trapping it tightly. This is one of the keys to the head and arm triangle. Rodrigo must keep Phillipe's arm trapped, and leave no space for Phillipe to counter by pulling the arm out to his left.

4 Rodrigo slides his right hand forward on the mat, and locks his left hand on his right biceps, completing the figure-four, with his arms around Phillipe's head and left arm. Rodrigo circles his right hand and places it on top of Phillipe's forehead. Rodrigo then applies the choking pressure by squeezing his arms and bringing his elbows together. At the same time, he drives his torso slightly forward and down. He makes sure not to push his weight forward. This would create a neck crank. Instead, he remembers the proper mechanics: to press his arms in, closing the elbows together.

Mounted attack: counter to the push

Being mounted by your opponent is extremely bad in a street fight or an NHB match. The person on top can throw punches at your face at will. Many times in a fight the person being mounted will extend both arms and push the chest of the attacker. Although it is a crude way to escape, it can be surprisingly effective if the person on top does not properly react to the push. In this case, Phillipe is pushing Rodrigo away to his own left. If Rodrigo doesn't react quickly, Phillipe can either roll Rodrigo over and end up in his guard or escape his hips to the right and start to replace the guard.

1 Rodrigo is mounted on Phillipe. Phillipe reacts by extending both arms, and pushing Rodrigo's chest up. Rodrigo reacts by leaning forward, and turning his shoulders clockwise to deflect the push.

2 Having deflected the initial thrust by Phillipe's arms, Rodrigo now looks for the submission. He wraps his right arm around both of Phillipe's hands, slides his left knee up towards Phillipe's head, plants his left hand out on the opposite side, and leans forward, pushing his hips against Phillipe's right shoulder. Notice that because of the use of the gloves, it makes it much harder for Phillipe to pull his arms from Rodrigo's right arm wrap.

3 Rodrigo continues to lean forward, bracing off his left arm as he slides his left shin over the right side of Phillipe's face. He drives his left knee down to the mat, making sure he leaves his left foot hooked around the back of Phillipe's neck. Notice that Rodrigo's right arm still has control over Phillipe's right arm, and Rodrigo's hips are going forward, pressing against Phillipe's elbow. Also note that Rodrigo has turned Phillipe over to his side effectively, by leaning forward and pulling on Phillipe's right arm. Again notice that the glove makes it very difficult for Phillipe to pull his hand out and free the arm.

4 To finish the lock, Rodrigo falls to the mat on his left side, closes his knees together, trapping the elbow, and taking away any space or chance for Phillipe to rotate the arm. Rodrigo further immobilizes Phillipe's right hand, by locking his own left arm around Phillipe's right arm, with Rodrigo's left hand holding his own right elbow. Rodrigo thrusts his hips forward and leans back with his shoulders for the arm lock. At this point, Phillipe's only escape may be to roll over his shoulders.

5 If Phillipe does not submit to the lock, and manages to roll forward over his shoulder, Rodrigo just follows him around. When Phillipe ends up with his back on the mat, the same armlock still applies.

5 Side view Notice how Rodrigo turns his shoulders to his right, and pulls Phillipe's arm across to the right, against his hips. Also, as Phillipe rolls to escape the lock, Rodrigo slides his right leg over Phillipe's head, to end up with his legs on each side of Phillipe's head for control.

Mounted attack: double attack

Throwing punches to the face from the mounted position generally gets good results. Either the opponent gets knocked out, or in his desperation to escape he will yield opportunities for submissions. In this situation, Rodrigo delivers a sequence of punches to Phillipe's face, Phillipe blocks, and Rodrigo takes that opportunity to go for the armlock.

1 Rodrigo is mounted on Phillipe. Phillipe has his elbows in, and his hands close to his face, to protect it from punches. Rodrigo cocks his right arm, in preparation of punching. Notice that if Rodrigo throws a direct punch, he will most likely hit Phillipe's glove.

2 Instead, Rodrigo raises his hips off Phillipe's stomach, swings his shoulders to the left, and throws a punch around Phillipe's left hand, striking his face. If Phillipe doesn't react, and tries to escape, Rodrigo can continue to punch at will, swinging his shoulders and looping the punches to Phillipe's face.

3 Phillipe extends both arms, pushing Rodrigo's chest straight up. Rodrigo counters by leaning forward and driving his hips forward. He keeps his chest straight, to deflect the push. However, Rodrigo allows a slight pressure against Phillipe's hands, in preparation for the armlock. If Rodrigo completely deflects Phillipe's hands off his chest, it would not only make the armlock a little more difficult, but also would eliminate the element of surprise.

4 **Alternate angle** Rodrigo can choose either of Phillipe's arms to armlock. In this case, he picks the right one. He slides his right hand between Phillipe's arms, touching his solar plexus. He also turns his own shoulders to the right, using his left arm to encircle Phillipe's right arm, until his left hand is on top of his right one. Notice that Rodrigo does not grab Phillipe's arm, but rather encircles it with his left arm. If he attempted to just grab the arm, Phillipe would notice the danger and pull his arm back, which would make it harder for the attack to succeed. The key here, as in most attacks, is for Rodrigo to set up the move without tipping off his opponent to the real danger. Rodrigo puts the weight of his body on his hands and uses them as pivot points.

5 Bracing off his arms and hands, Rodrigo pivots his body around to the right. His left leg spins around Phillipe's head. Notice that Rodrigo's hips lean forward, pushing against Phillipe's right elbow. The key to a good armlock from the mount is to be able to swing the legs and body around smoothly. To do so, you must practice. Remember to lean forward and to use your arms as both support and pivot points. Having successfully spun around Phillipe's right arm, Rodrigo traps the arm as he falls back to the mat with the armlock in place. Notice that Rodrigo uses both hands to grab Phillipe's right wrist. Again, because of the hands, Rodrigo has a lot of control over Phillipe's hand. This makes it difficult for him to escape by twisting the arm or pulling it out.

Back attack: armlock

Many times when you have your opponent's back, he is so closed up that there aren't many options of attack. In this case, Rodrigo has one hook and is attempting to place the second hook, but Phillipe defends by making himself into a ball with the left elbow inside the knee. Rodrigo uses a clever method to prod the opening and attack the arm. Note that this attack works from the complete back mount (both hooks in) as well as (with a minor adjustment) the turtle position.

1 Rodrigo is on Phillipe's back, with his right foot hooked in. Notice that Phillipe covers himself with his left elbow inside the knee, preventing Rodrigo from placing the left foot hook. Rodrigo maintains control of the back by grabbing Phillipe's left side with his left hand, and by bracing off his straight right arm. Notice that Rodrigo's right knee is on the ground, just behind Phillipe's right elbow, which keeps the right elbow slightly open.

2 Rodrigo spins his head and torso to his right, and drives his left hand around, in front of the right side of Phillipe's head, until it touches his right knee. At the same time, he plants his left foot wide, to Phillipe's left, and pushes off it.

3 Rodrigo rolls over to his left side, while at the same time using his right arm to hook around Phillipe's right leg. He pulls Phillipe over with the arm, pulling the right leg as he rolls over his left side of the body. Notice that Rodrigo's left leg is near Phillipe's head. Rodrigo uses this leg to push Phillipe's head, forcing him to roll, and causing his body to follow.

3 **Reverse angle** Notice how Rodrigo hooks Phillipe's right leg, by wrapping his right arm around the outside of the right knee. Also notice how Rodrigo turns his right knee up to the top, changing the angle of the leg so that his right foot and shin can aid in the reversal.

4 Rodrigo uses his right leg to help bring Phillipe around; he kicks his heel back, pushing his calf against Phillipe's stomach. Notice that Rodrigo's left arm controls Phillipe's right arm. Notice also that by controlling Phillipe's right leg with his right arm hooked around it, Rodrigo prevents Phillipe from posting it for an attempt to either escape the armlock attack, or to defend the reversal.

4 **Reverse angle** As he turns Phillipe over, Rodrigo's right foot hook releases and his entire lower leg pushes against Phillipe's stomach. At the same time, Rodrigo kicks his heel toward the ground. Rodrigo ends up with control over Phillipe's right leg and arm.

5 Rodrigo loops his left leg over Phillipe's head, and applies the armlock by leaning to his right and extending Phillipe's right arm. He also pushes his hips against the elbow joint. Notice that Rodrigo used his right arm, which was hooked around Phillipe's leg, to help pull himself around to the right.

Back attack: trapping the arm

Being on someone's back is one of the best positions to be in, whether you are competing in jiu-jitsu, submission grappling, or NHB. In an NHB match, however, because of the gloves, it is much easier for the opponent to defend chokes. He can grab the gloves, and it is also harder to slide a gloved hand under someone's neck. Because of that constraint, NHB fighters have developed a series of ways to expose the opponent's neck. Here is one of Rodrigo's favorites: trapping the arm.

1 Rodrigo is on Phillipe's back, but Phillipe has a good defensive position, with both arms crossed under his neck. His hands are open, blocking Rodrigo's hands from coming in at both sides of his neck. Seeing that Phillipe has his right arm over the left, Rodrigo will attack the right arm.

2 With his left hand, Rodrigo attacks Phillipe's neck as he attempts to slide the arm around the neck for a choke. This causes a distraction and brings Phillipe's attention to that side. Because the right arm is over the left, Phillipe's right elbow is further away from his body. Rodrigo uses his left hand to push down on Phillipe's right hand, forcing the elbow further away from the body. This creates a space where Rodrigo can slide his right hand in. Notice that Rodrigo's hand slides just under Phillipe's right elbow, and grabs Phillipe's right wrist.

3 Once he has control over Phillipe's right wrist, Rodrigo pushes it down to open it up.

4 Rodrigo falls to the mat as he slides his hips out to his right, and loops his right leg over Phillipe's right arm. Rodrigo uses his right hand to push Phillipe's right arm open and out.

5 Rodrigo locks his right leg over Phillipe's right arm, making sure to trap it over his forearm and lock the gloved hand in. At this point, Rodrigo has to release his right arm quickly; otherwise, the glove will prevent him from freeing the arm. Notice that Rodrigo's heel touches the top of his glove to keep the trap around Phillipe's arm and to allow Rodrigo the ability to release his hand from under the arm. Rodrigo uses his heel to push and drive his gloved right hand out. Rodrigo is ready to attack Phillipe's neck, with two hands against one defending hand.

6 **Incorrect** If Rodrigo waits until his heel presses down on Phillipe's arm, the gloves will prevent him from pulling his hand, and the hand will be trapped.

Back attack: arm drag over the face

If your opponent traps your hand while you are on his back, you need to push the opponent's hand away and create the space to pry your gloved hand out and follow with a rear naked choke. Normally in a jiu-jitsu or a grappling match, fighters rely on technique and finesse to submit their opponents; however, since NHB is a violent game, it allows for a few more direct and even brutal moves to open up opportunities. In this case, Rodrigo drives his forearm into Phillipe's nose, causing a lot of discomfort and creating the opening for the choke.

1 Rodrigo is on Phillipe's back, and Phillipe is trapping Rodrigo's right hand with his right arm. With his left hand, Rodrigo pushes down on Phillipe's right hand, forcing it down and creating the space necessary to release his right hand.

2 Rodrigo yanks his right hand out; the movement causes his arm to swing wide. Rodrigo resorts to a little less finesse. Rodrigo moves his right arm in, as if he was going to punch Phillipe's face, and then drives his forearm over Phillipe's nose, as if he were trying to punch an object next to Phillipe's left ear. Rodrigo, dragging the forearm over Phillipe's nose, forces Phillipe's head back and opens up the neck. As Phillipe leans back to relieve the pain on his face, notice that Rodrigo posts his left arm back, to keep him from falling to the mat.

3 Having exposed Phillipe's neck, Rodrigo drives his left hand across the neck, making sure his hand goes all the way around and out to the right side. He also makes sure that his left elbow is centered in front of Phillipe's neck.

4 Rodrigo starts to lock the choke by falling to his left, and sliding his right hand behind Phillipe's head. Notice that by falling to his left, Rodrigo makes it more difficult for Phillipe to escape the choke. Normally, Phillipe would want to escape away from the elbow that is choking him; in this case, he would escape to the right. Also notice that Rodrigo first slides his right hand behind Phillipe's head, before locking his left hand over his right biceps. He does that because he does not want Phillipe to be able to grab his glove and block the completion of the choke. If he were to first grab the right biceps with the left hand, Rodrigo would actually leave the gloved right hand slightly out, giving Phillipe an opportunity to grab and block it.

5 Rodrigo locks a "mata leao" choke, with his left hand grabbing his right biceps. He applies pressure by closing his left arm as if he were doing a bicep curl, while bringing his elbows together and pulling the arms in for the choke. Notice that because he is choking with the left arm, Rodrigo has his head on the right side of Phillipe's head.

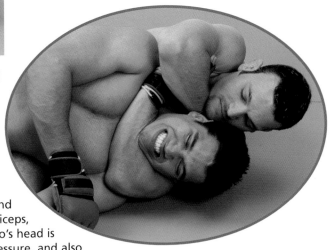

5 Detail Notice that Rodrigo's left arm is wrapped around Phillipe's neck, with his left hand grabbing his right biceps, and his right hand locked behind his head. Also, Rodrigo's head is on the right side of Phillipe's head, in order to apply pressure, and also to prevent Phillipe from turning his head.

GROUND FIGHTING

Knee-on-Stomach

The knee-on-stomach opens many options for attacking in an NHB match. By mixing in strikes and pressing your knee on your opponent's stomach, you will generate a lot of opportunities to finish the match by either submission or knockout as your opponent desperately tries to escape the position. The constant pressure of the knee-on-stomach will wear down even the most fit opponent. It is important to remain agile and ready to quickly adjust to any changes in your opponent's position by changing the knee pressure or rotating from side to side. It is also important to keep distance between your chest and your opponent's chest to prevent him from grabbing your head and pulling you down.

Knee-on-stomach attack: punches to armlock

The knee-on-stomach is a great position for an NHB fighter to deliver strikes from. Because of its mobility, you are able to adapt to the opponent's counters or escape attempts, quickly opening up submissions. In this case, Rodrigo starts causing panic in Phillipe by delivering a barrage of punches, then follows with an armlock.

1 Rodrigo has his knee on Phillipe's stomach, and hits him repeatedly with punches to the face.

2 Phillipe attempts to escape the position. He plants his right foot out, and pushes off it as he tries to turn to his left. He wants to get on his side, and then on his knees, as he hooks Rodrigo's left leg with his right arm. This keeps Rodrigo from turning, or spinning around, as he evades the knee. Rodrigo stops the motion by putting his left hand on Phillipe's right shoulder, and applying enough of his weight on that arm to stop Phillipe from turning. Rodrigo will use this hand as a bracing point.

3 Rodrigo reaches with his right hand, and grabs Phillipe's right wrist, to prevent him from pulling it back.

4 Rodrigo pivots his body around his left foot in such a way that his legs frame Phillipe's right arm. Notice that Rodrigo's right hand remains in control of Phillipe's right hand. To prepare for the armlock, Rodrigo bends his knees as he starts to sit down on the mat next to the right side of Phillipe's body. At this point, Rodrigo's body position is perfect for the armlock.

5 After his buttocks hit the ground, Rodrigo leans back and pulls Phillipe's right arm out. He also drives his hips against Phillipe's right elbow, for the armlock.

Knee-on-stomach attack: punches to triangle

Another great opportunity that occurs when punching from the knee-on-stomach is the triangle. In this case, the opponent attempts to escape the knee-on-stomach by pushing the attacker's hips with his inside arm (closest to the attacker), which is the perfect setup for the triangle.

1 Rodrigo has his knee on Phillipe's stomach, and he is punching Phillipe's face. Phillipe uses his inside arm to push away Rodrigo's hip, in an attempt to escape the position.

2 Pivoting off his right foot, Rodrigo turns his body in a clockwise direction, and brings his left leg around so that his knee is on Phillipe's stomach, making sure his shin is over Phillipe's right biceps.

3 Rodrigo continues to spin, sliding the knee on Phillipe's stomach, and he drives his left knee over Phillipe's right arm, trapping it over the biceps for a new pivot point.

3 Reverse angle Notice how Rodrigo traps Phillipe's right arm with his left leg. His knee, along with the foot on either side of the arm, ensures that Phillipe cannot pull the arm and escape the attack. Rodrigo plants his left hand on Phillipe's right hip, to help him turn, and to keep Phillipe from turning to his left and escaping. Rodrigo makes sure that his knee is on the ground, trapping Phillip's arm. Also, Rodrigo's left hand is on Phillipe's right hip. Rodrigo will use that hand to propel himself and spin around.

4 Rodrigo continues to spin in a clockwise direction, pivoting off the left knee as he circles his right leg over and around Phillipe's head. As his right leg reaches near Phillipe's head, Rodrigo's pivot point changes from the left knee to his buttocks, so that he can sit on Phillipe's stomach. As he changes his pivot point, Rodrigo takes his left knee off the mat and uses his left heel to help his motion. Notice that Rodrigo makes as wide a circle as possible, so he can trap Phillipe's left arm inside his right leg as he ends the spin. Rodrigo uses his right hand to drive Phillipe's left arm to the side. Rodrigo ends his spin by sitting on Phillipe's stomach, with Phillipe's head and left arm trapped between his legs.

5 With both hands, Rodrigo pulls up on Phillipe's head and left arm, and slides his left heel under Phillipe's neck, until he can reach his left ankle with his right hand. From here, he can lock the figure-four around Phillipe's head and left arm. Rodrigo leans to his left to make it easier to slide his leg under Phillipe's neck.

6 Rodrigo rolls to his left, bringing Phillipe up on top of him. He uses that motion to lock his right leg over his left foot, securing the triangle.

7 Rodrigo ends the roll on the bottom, with Phillipe in his triangle.

Knee-on-stomach attack: punches to triangle (opponent blocks the leg)

A common occurrence when using the previous technique to transition from the punches to the triangle is for the opponent to raise his arm or simply by accident have the arm up, stopping the attacker's leg from circling over and around the outside arm, thereby taking away the triangle. In that case, Rodrigo quickly continues his transition and goes for a choke. We pick up the position from step 91.3, when Rodrigo traps the arm with his leg.

1 Rodrigo has trapped Phillipe's right arm with his left leg.

2 He sits on Phillipe's stomach, and continues turning his body, while bringing his right leg around, circling over Phillipe's head. This time, however, he cannot go around Phillipe's left arm, because it is bent upward. Rodrigo cannot go for the triangle from here, because neither of Phillipe's arms is inside Rodrigo's legs. At this point, Phillipe will attempt to escape by pushing Rodrigo's left leg away, as he escapes his hips to his right.

3 Pushing off his left hand, which has been firmly planted on Phillipe's right hip to try to prevent Phillipe from turning to his left and into him, Rodrigo continues his body rotation. He brings his left leg all the way around and over Phillipe's head, until it is on the left side. Phillipe escapes as he turns to his left, and he uses his right hand to drive Rodrigo's left leg to his left, away from him. Notice that Rodrigo uses his left hand and right foot as balance points for the move.

4 Rodrigo lands with his left hip on the mat, and with his body on the opposite side of where he started in relation to Phillipe. At this point, normally Phillipe would still be struggling to turn to his left, and fighting with Rodrigo for position. Rodrigo immediately wraps the right arm around Phillipe's neck, and presses his chest against Phillipe's right shoulder. This prevents Phillipe from turning to his knees. Notice how Rodrigo traps Phillipe's right elbow with his chest, forcing the right arm across the body in a very uncomfortable position.

5 Rodrigo brings his left elbow in against Phillipe's back, so that his arm is perpendicular to Phillipe's back. This prevents Phillipe from turning back. By scissoring his legs, he also switches his hips, so they are facing the mat. Rodrigo's left hand locks with his right hand, so that his palms are touching each other. Rodrigo makes sure to keep his chest tight against Phillipe's to keep the right arm trapped. Rodrigo now has the choke in place.

6 Rodrigo brings his knees in and applies the choking pressure, with his right biceps pressing against Phillipe's throat. At the same time, he drives Phillipe's right arm with his chest, pressing it up against the throat as well. Rodrigo brings his knees in to apply pressure. Should Rodrigo keep his legs out, he would allow Phillipe to try to turn back to his left, and he would reduce the choking pressure. It is important for Rodrigo to maintain Phillipe's back flat on the ground.

6 **Side view** Notice how Rodrigo's hands are clasped together, with the right forearm pressing against the back of Phillipe's neck. Rodrigo's chest drives up, forcing Phillipe's right arm to push against his own throat.

Armlock from knee-on-stomach: variation

The knee-on-stomach offers a great deal of possibilities for strikes and submissions in an NHB match. Rodrigo really likes this combination, which delivers the punishment with a barrage of punches and, when the opponent tries to block the punches, goes for the armlock. This time Rodrigo attacks the inside arm as Phillipe tries to block the punches instead of turning into Rodrigo as he did in technique 90.

1 Rodrigo has his right knee on Phillipe's stomach, and is delivering a barrage of punches from this position.

2 Phillipe turns to his left and stretches his right arm, trying to block Rodrigo's punches and to push him away as well. Rodrigo continues to punch down with his left hand.

3 Rodrigo wraps his right arm around Phillipe's right arm and pulls it forward, further turning Phillipe. He drives his hips forward, and pushes Phillipe's face down with his straight left arm. This keeps Phillipe from sitting up. Putting his weight on his right knee and left hand, Rodrigo pivots on his right leg. He circles his left leg around Phillipe's head, until his foot lands in front of Phillipe's face. Notice how tightly Rodrigo's hips are pushing against Phillipe's right arm; this will remove any space, and prevent Phillipe from pulling the arm out.

4 As soon as his left foot touches the mat, Rodrigo sits down and falls to the mat, making sure he sits as close to Phillipe's right shoulder as possible. He then arches back with his torso, and extends Phillipe's right arm. He also drives his hips up for the armlock, hyperextending the elbow.

Armlock counter to omoplata

Continuing from the previous technique, Rodrigo has Phillipe in an armlock. One of the defenses to the armlock is to bridge and roll. This is a last-resort escape and should only be used when you have no choice and feel you are able to spin your hand so that your elbow rotates away from the attacker's hips. In NHB this is especially difficult to execute because the gloves allow tremendous control over the hand and the arm, making it very difficult to turn. Be extremely careful when trying this type of escape, as you may twist and damage your elbow if the attacker maintains stiff control of your hand. However, at times the execution is perfect and one can escape the armlock. If your opponent should escape your armlock in this manner, immediately change to the omoplata, as Rodrigo does here.

1 Rodrigo has Phillipe in an armlock, with his right arm extended. Phillipe is able to turn his wrist, and bridges up over his left shoulder. He turns over to his right by looping his right leg over. Rodrigo still maintains control over Phillipe's arm, with both hands gripping the wrist.

2 As Phillipe gets to all fours, Rodrigo pushes Phillipe's right wrist to his left side and circles his torso to his left. He then loops his left leg around Phillipe's right arm and continues to push Phillipe's wrist, bending the arm and locking the omoplata hold.

3 Rodrigo sits up, reaching with his left arm over Phillipe's back, until he grabs the left hip. This prevents Phillipe from rolling forward and escaping the omoplata. Rodrigo continues to circle his legs around to his right, applying pressure with his hips.

3 Reverse angle Rodrigo circles his legs around to his right. Notice that they are bent at the knees; angling back makes it easy for Rodrigo to drive his hips forward and to apply the pressure to Phillipe's right shoulder. Rodrigo then drives Phillipe's right hand toward his right ear, torquing the shoulder.